ZEN
IN THE ART OF
CLIMBING
MOUNTAINS

Travellers will cross many rivers and climb many mountains
Plainsmen may always live within a single valley
But only those seeking truth will ever reach the summit.

11th Century Indian Saying. Anon

ZEN IN THE ART OF CLIMBING MOUNTAINS

NEVILLE SHULMAN

CHARLES E. TUTTLE COMPANY
Boston • Rutland, Vermont • Tokyo

Published in the United States in 1992 by
Charles E. Tuttle Company, Inc. of Rutland, Vermont & Tokyo, Japan,
with editorial offices at 77 Central Street, Boston, Massachusetts 02109.

Library of Congress Cataloging-in-Publication Data

Shulman, Neville, 1945-
  Zen in the art of climbing mountains / Neville Shulman.
    p.   cm.
  Includes bibliographical references.
  ISBN 0-8048-1775-8
  1. Shulman, Neville, 1945- . 2. Mountaineers—Great Britain
—Biography. 3. Zen Buddhism. 4. Mountaineering—Blanc, Mont
(France and Italy). 5. Blanc, Mont (France and Italy)—Description
and travel. I. Title.
GV199.92.S55A3 1992
  796.5'22'092—dc20
  [B]   91-67335
                                                         CIP

Fifty percent of the royalties
earned by the writer of this book
are donated to children's charities.

Cover design by Fahrenheit
PRINTED IN THE UNITED STATES

Zen in the Art of Climbing Mountains is dedicated to those who reached with me for the Summit of Mont Blanc, and also to those who, over many years, have encouraged me to climb many mountains, especially when my steps have faltered. My thanks to John B, Jan, Andrew, Duncan, John C, Jonathan, Iwan, Jim, Ian, Matt, Rebecca, Jane, Nigel, Tony, Ridley, Lesley, George, John G, Jackie, Sigmund, Donald, Lela.

FOREWORD

We mountaineers are a strange bunch of individualists and I am pleased to welcome Neville Shulman as one of our number. After you climb your first mountain, as Neville Shulman has with Mont Blanc, you are invariably hooked forever, and will spend countless hours dreaming and planning for the next mountain. In fact, I understand by the time this book is published he will have attempted to climb, back-to-back (no mean feat), two further mountains: Mt. Kilimanjaro (the highest in Africa) and Mt. Kenya (a tough and technical climb, particularly the last 2,000 feet). I knew when reading this book that he would continue his mountaineering and that he had breathed deeply of the spirit of the mountains.

During any climb we all have to fight those demons lurking on the mountain itself and those inside our minds; *Zen in the Art of Climbing Mountains* explains very cogently the philosophy which helped Neville Shulman to the summit. It is a philosophy, under whatever name, that we all, in part at least, need if we are to climb any mountain.

When you are climbing, struggling really, to reach your goal for that day, everything else must be put aside, otherwise your determination might flag and on the mountain that can be disastrous. I've really enjoyed this book and it has made me realise again how very different mountaineers can be, one to another, and the many different approaches and styles we all have.

Chris Bonington

CONTENTS

	Preface	ix
1	Mountains and Mountaineers	3
2	High Peaks and Altitudes	5
3	Zen Decision	9
4	Mind and Body	15
5	July 1 – Journey to Base Camp	22
6	July 2 – Pains and Preparations	28
7	The Way of the Mountain	32
8	First Abseil	36
9	First Glacier	40
10	July 3 – Learning Rope	50
11	July 4 – Ascend the Needle, across to the Tacul	58
12	Sixteen hours in the ice	62
13	July 5 – Trekking back through a blizzard	68
14	Spirit of *shin*	73
15	July 6 – Ascent to the Tête Rousse	77
16	July 7 – The Mountain speaks	83
17	July 8 – Anxious times at the Refuge du Goûter	87
18	July 9 – Final Ascent	95

19   Feeling the Summit   101

20   Descending the Glaciers   106

       Bibliography   116

PREFACE

Everyday all of us have to attempt a mountain of sorts. For some it is just getting out of bed; others need help to do even that. One of my main interests and fields of activities is working in children's charities, and many of the children these charities assist are from very deprived backgrounds. The children are often handicapped as well, and sometimes the children are multi-deprived and multi-handicapped. Everyday they must attempt to climb their own mountains. Their resources constantly amaze me and it's always refreshing and uplifting to witness the efforts of those who, even faced with seemingly impossible odds, are prepared to tackle their daily mountains and try to overcome extreme obstacles and tremendous challenges. Theatre is also a great love, particularly Shakespeare, whose plays contain so many Zen thoughts, and I rarely visit one of the charities and see the pain and the hope etched deeply in those young and old faces, without thinking of the words of Prince Hamlet 'to suffer the slings and arrows of outrageous fortune'. Those that refuse to give up and are always willing to struggle uphill, can truly call themselves mountaineers, certainly in my Zen sense of the word. If I am asked what does Zen mean, although no definition should or can really or readily be given or accepted. I might reply 'Zen equals effort but remains effortless. Zen is not judgemental but expects everything'. What that means and what I mean by it one should not try to explain further, but I do have a feeling that those who should know, do know.

I decided to climb the mountain first; that must always be the first decision. After that commitment, certainly to emphasise it and prevent any weakening of spirit, I then decided that my climb must benefit the children who have given and continue to give me so many wonderful insights and such immeasurable benefits. I asked colleagues and friends, and their friends, to sponsor my climb for as many feet or metres as they thought they could. There was a really magnificent response and I am very grateful to those who enabled a substantial sum to be raised, which in turn has been used to help those children who are abused, deprived, handicapped and, very sadly, often all three. It is only fair that this book will also continue to help this very important and vital work.

When I was young, very young, I remember reading a book, sadly now lost, that told the story of a rather strange old man who lived at the top of a particularly high mountain. This man knew the answers to all the questions; all you had to do was climb the mountain and ask him. I always wanted to find the old man before I grew too old myself and ask him my own questions.

Very many years later I dreamed about a high snow-white mountain, and at the very top, waiting, was the same old man from my childhood. He did not appear to be any older. He was smiling and beckoning to me. He seemed very far off and it was a long way to climb, but immediately and unhesitatingly I started my ascent. When I awoke I still had not reached the mountain's summit, but somehow I felt very content. I knew there was time, on another day, to finish the climb.

1

MOUNTAINS AND MOUNTAINEERS

Mountains have always been magical and special places, often illustrated as mistily shrouded and portrayed as full of extreme mysteries. The gods lived on them; many kings built their castles and fortresses there; the ordinary people were usually forbidden access to them. Even to this day there is still one called Machhapuchhare (the Fishtail), the sacred mountain of Nepal, which no one is permitted to climb; Nepalese law actually decrees death as the punishment for anyone's disobedience. Throughout the centuries mountains have exerted powerful influences on our imaginations, and, rightly so, many countries treat their own mountains as unique national treasures. A Hindu text from the *Devistrotra* states that 'So long as this land will have mountains and forests, so long will this Earth survive'.

Mountaineers are a very unusual breed of people. Experienced mountaineers decide to set out to climb a mountain, and from that moment, and at that time, everything else within their ordinary lives becomes secondary and of lesser consequence. Only what and where they are now, at whatever point they may be in their preparation or on the ascent, means anything to them. All that really matters is only how they will react to the mountain and how the mountain will react to them. They purposely divest themselves of everything that is unnecessary, and at the commencement of the climb they stand before the mountain naked of their material wealth, authority and influence. The mountain alone holds and owns the power.

Not so surprising as it may at first seem, many women can be as equally committed as men to the testing activity of mountain climbing. The qualities and traits needed for mountain climbing are many, but foremost amongst them are tenacity and courage, and a woman possessing these attributes will certainly be equal to any man in her determination to climb and to succeed.

2

HIGH PEAKS AND ALTITUDES

Mountaineers who venture into the harsh weather conditions that can shroud the high peaks expose themselves to a number of potential physical problems.

Human beings are warm-blooded, and need to maintain a constant body temperature. This is achieved by balancing the body's heat production and its heat loss. Heat is produced in the body, both as a result of the many chemical reactions that occur as part of our normal metabolism, and as a side-effect of the use of our muscles. This is why, when we get cold, we automatically start to shiver – the muscles start to contract involuntarily and, as a byproduct, generate a certain amount of heat.

Heat is lost from the body's surface. When we are cold the blood vessels near the surface tend to shut down automatically, so that blood carrying heat from the deeper tissues cannot get near the surface of the body and cool down – this has the effect of conserving heat, despite the fact that we may look blue with cold. Conversely, if we get very hot the surface vessels dilate, allowing blood to transport heat from the deeper tissues and lose it at the body's surface. The sweat glands also become very active, cooling the body down as the sweat evaporates from the skin's surface.

If the balance between heat gain and heat loss is upset a number of strange physiological and mental responses begin to appear – the body and mind go a little bit haywire. And the extreme conditions of weather that occur on mountains can very easily upset the body's heat balance if the mountaineer is not well prepared, added to which, the exertion of carrying a heavy back-pack can induce physical and mental fatigue and can further undermine the climber's ability to cope.

Then there is the third potential problem, that of altitude sickness. Usually from approximately 3,500 metres (around 11,500 feet) upwards, the thinness of the air and consequent lack of oxygen will cause many mountaineers to suffer from altitude sickness – shortness of breath, dizziness, even nausea and confusion. This is why the highest and most famous mountain in the world, Mount Everest, usually cannot be climbed successfully and unsupported without the benefit of oxygen supplies.

However, what is probably the second most famous mountain, Mont Blanc, the highest in Western Europe does not necessarily require a mountaineer to carry oxygen on his or her climb to its Summit. But because it is the most attempted mountain in the world, invariably more accidents and more

Seven of the highest peaks of the seven continents of the world			
Everest	(Nepal)	8,848 metres	(29,028 feet)
McKinley	(Alaska)	6,194 metres	(20,320 feet)
Kilimanjaro	(Tanzania)	5,895 metres	(19,340 feet)
Popocatatepetl	(Mexico)	5,410 metres	(17,749 feet)
Carstensz	(New Guinea)	4,884 metres	(16,023 feet)
Vinson	(Antarctica)	4,868 metres	(15,970 feet)
Mont Blanc	(France)	4,807 metres	(15,771 feet)

fatalities occur there each year than on any other mountain, and each climber, no matter how experienced, must always treat it with the total respect it unreservedly deserves. Indeed each and every mountain is cloaked in its own dangers and offers its own perilous and special conflicts. There are always unknown forces to contest and confront. The elements can quickly transform a moment in time to a moment lost for ever. Even Britain's highest mountain, Ben Nevis, 1,342 metres (4,404 feet), although not in the major league of great climbing mountains, can itself overwhelm the experienced mountaineer, and it too annually claims the lives of those who neglect to prepare properly in body and mind to meet its always present hostilities. The mystical Mount Fuji, 3,776 metres (12,388 feet), is the highest Japanese mountain, but its exquisite beauty can mask an awesome force, which it can unleash in a moment against the ill-prepared or unguarded climber.

As long as mountains exist, so there will be those who need to climb to their summits. As long as there are those who are prepared to strive against and attempt to defeat the unknown, whatever that may be or represent, so there will be personal mountains to climb. Two of the greatest of the world's mountaineers, whose joint courage and spirit burn brightly in mountaineering lore, are Mallory and Irving. They died attempting to reach the Summit of Mount Everest in 1924. And it was Mallory who, when asked before his last heroic and historic attempt why he wanted to climb Everest, made the famous statement, 'Because It Is There' – a statement that is quintessential Zen.

3

ZEN DECISION

I have no prior climbing or mountain experience, apart from skiing, and I feel that only a love of snow and an appreciation of the majesty of mountains creates any link between two such vastly different activities. Unfortunately, and just as importantly as I am subsequently to discover, I have also absolutely no knowledge of the rock and ice techniques that are needed and used in completing any snow-mountain climb. But what I do have, above all, is my dream, and when I learn about a small climbing group being organised to attempt an ascent of Mont Blanc, that most romantic of the high mountains, I apply immediately to join the team. I do not volunteer my lack of involvement in any previous climbing expeditions, and in the brief application form I complete I mostly emphasize my participation in a short journey in 1989 through the Arctic to reach the North Pole. I do not explain that it was as part of a modern art team to witness and record the creation of transient ice sculptures by a contemporary British artist; nor that we flew to the Pole, hopping from one remote airstrip to another, in small Twin Otter aeroplanes. Over that seven-day journey I probably spent altogether some 60 exhausting and often frightening hours in the air as we sometimes had to battle fierce wind currents, so at least the trip was in some way a test of my stamina.

I feel very happy indeed when I receive the letter confirming I am accepted, and read through the brief notes of information and instructions. The informality of this letter and the lack of more vigorous questioning of my mountaineering abilities puzzles me somewhat, but I am really too excited to question the invitation, and just count myself lucky to be included. Much, much later I am able to understand, and this understanding underlines the affinity that I now know exists between mountain climbing and Zen. I realise that all mountaineers are always expected, ultimately, to place their total reliance on their own personal judgment as to whether or not to climb and what potential risks are likely to be faced.

However, after the first few days of euphoria, the realisation of what I am about to undertake sets in. I know I need to confront my fears, to prepare my mind and to reach some calmness of spirit. Detachment and self liberation, the turning inwards, does not happen by mere chance: it has to be sought. I need to feel my total presence, assertive and committed to my decision. So I walk into the nearby woods and, after strolling for some while through the trees and running my hands across the roughness of their different barks, I finally come across a solitary, silver beech, set within a circled, rough terrain, the tree's highest branches reaching symbolically skywards, and I stop to sit at its base. It is mid-afternoon. I cannot see anyone else around, and after a short while of mental adjustment and intense thought it wouldn't matter to me whether anyone does come by and observes me sitting there.

Zen in its simplest Japanese form stands for and means meditation, being an attempt to translate and equal the Sanskrit word for meditation, *dhyana*. The Zen philosophy itself originated first in India, then was introduced into China and finally entered Japan in the 14th century. Within Zen, as it is practised today, the concentrated or deep meditation that it teaches, and Zen followers practise, is called Zazen. It is preferable, but not absolutely necessary, to carry out the practice of Zazen in the lotus sitting position, one's body securely and firmly anchored, but a skiing accident the previous year has temporarily stiffened one of my knees and, as it is responding very slowly to treatment, the lotus position is still proving impossible for me. So I sit straight back against the hardness of the tree, and stretch both my legs flatly forward, thus forming two parallel lines.

First of all I argue myself through the reasons for not attempting the Mont Blanc climb. They are powerful and completely logical, and cannot be easily faulted. I am a complete novice at mountain climbing. I have no technical knowledge. I do not train very regularly, and certainly not extensively. The others in the team are likely to be experienced climbers and may resent my participation, and I might hold them back. Even if I become fitter and stronger it is unlikely I will be able to achieve my objective of reaching the Summit. Anything less than that would not be acceptable and it would be considered a failure.

Thus the only real argument I can put forward for going ahead is that I desperately want to. I am not even certain of all my reasons, but I hope I will learn these during the ascent.

I think for a moment I am crying; water is trickling down my face. In fact it has started raining and I haven't noticed. I realise the sky has become quite dark. I begin to get up and leave, still with my decision not fully resolved, but in that same moment accept that I shouldn't move. It is going to be so much tougher on the mountain. I will be challenged by more extreme and harsher elements; I will have to fight through under very arduous conditions if I expect to have any chance of succeeding. After a lengthy time of further introspection I finally conclude that the lack of an answer is in fact the answer. It is as if the rain has stopped, although it hasn't, but I feel the sun warming my face.

A koan is a question, usually given by a Zen master, that cannot be answered with the rational mind. I realise that I myself must not look for an immediate answer in this case, but should accept that I will allow the mountain and my presence on the mountain to answer me; I will make the climb and then I shall learn whether I should have gone at all. I stand up next to the silver beech and clasp my hands around its slender trunk. They slide smoothly down and it feels reassuring. It has stopped raining. The ground is wet except for the faint outlines of my legs.

There is a slight breeze against my face as I start back.

This non-reasoning – at least my postponing of any answer until I have passed a point of no return as far as starting the climb – proves subsequently somewhat unnerving. It means that I constantly have to battle against my doubts and the many fears that often present themselves unexpectedly during my ordinary and daily activities. I lean on some words of Bazo, a great Zen philosopher: 'Zen is the everyday mind, used as a means of helping to keep the inner thoughts balanced and tranquil.' Bazo died in 788 AD, and the fact that we don't know his age and his birth date is somehow rather reassuring, and helps to lend deeper significance to the straightforward message within his words.

At times in Zen it is important to try and obtain a state of mind known as *mushin*. The word is formed of two words, *mu* meaning empty or void and *shin* meaning mind or spirit. In experiencing and feeling *mushin* you can deal with and resolve the mental pressures that otherwise might overwhelm your peace of mind. I shall refer to *shin* subsequently as it is of the most vital importance in any activity or sport, and can play the greatest part in someone gaining supremacy over an obstacle or opponent that otherwise would be completely unassailable or unbeatable.

Gradually, as the days go by, I feel myself becoming more and more detached from my surroundings and any pressures that are being brought to bear. My mind sometimes reaches a plain of such quietness and withdrawal that it prevents the problems that sometimes occur having any impact on my consciousness and thought processes. The Zen master Foyan stated 'All

Zen practice requires detachment from thought. This is the way to save energy. Just detach yourself from emotional thought and understand there is no objective world. Then you will know how to practise Zen.'

4

MIND AND BODY

For some time I hug the knowledge of my planned mountain attempt to myself, still tussling both with the uncertainty it has created within me and the thought of the extreme testing I know it will subsequently cause. Eventually I share the decision with my family, my friends and my colleagues, and I learn a great deal from their different reactions. Very few are supportive. Most are incredulous, and many try actively to discourage me; they tell me 'You are too inexperienced' 'You are too old to start climbing at this stage', 'You have too many responsibilities to take such risks.' Most think that there is no way I can make it to the top.

Their discouragements have exactly the opposite effect on me to that expected; they firm up any wavering convictions I still have and help me to resolve my determination to continue. I will definitely go ahead. I will persevere no matter what. However, I do listen to their well-meant opinions as if I will continue to give consideration to them. But in my heart, although most of what they say makes sense, I know they will not sway me. I know something none of them know about me. I am going to climb Mont Blanc with my mind, my spirit, as well as with my feet. I will be putting into practice the Zen I have thought and tried to practise, with varying results, over so many years. Now I will learn the answers to the questions that have always troubled me. Could I? Would I? Even when the way becomes hostile and extremely painful? If I can carry my Zen with me and use it to contest the mountain, it means it will help me to climb other mountains, not only Mont Blanc; indeed I can battle against those mountains that pretend to be otherwise. We should all know a mountain disguises itself in many forms and uses many aliases. Some people have to climb their own mountains every day.

My first essential act is to defeat the bad karma that is being projected at me, albeit unwittingly, by those who are expecting me to fail. 'Don't worry,' I respond to them, 'I have no intention of pushing myself physically too far. If I find I am becoming too exhausted and I've driven myself beyond my capabilities, I will just give up and come down.' That seems to satisfy the doubters, and I am then mainly left alone to complete my preparations. I don't tell anyone that I will accept no limits and will not contemplate the prospect of failure, of defeat, on the mountain. For similar reasons I also reject the suggestion of some well-meaning friends, that perhaps I should start my climbing challenges first on a smaller mountain. I know that if I ever accept the possibility of defeat by Mont Blanc I will lose the inner strength I am gathering within me, and that is whispering gentle but positive encouragement and self-belief into my ears throughout my spiritual preparations.

Although never contemplating failure or defeat on the mountain, I know that to increase the overall chances in my favour I will have to train very thoroughly. I must make certain, given the limited time and opportunities I have, that my legs and my body will be as fit as possible for the contest that lies ahead. Any sporting individual who sets out and expects to win must train strongly and aggressively within the limitations set down by the restrictions of their normal lives.

Whilst skiing the previous year I had torn some ligaments in my left knee. There is still a loss of some mobility, and it is quite painful when my leg is stretched to any unnatural position. Of course, I know that my mountain climbing will do exactly that. But while I am prepared to put up with any pains that might be caused, I want to limit their effects as far as possible. So I increase my physiotherapy treatments, and my knee seems to improve. I am impatient to commence some physical training, but am warned to continue to rest my knee, as too much use too early on could delay its recovery and cause further strain, and it will then not stand up to the rigours of the mountain. Eventually I feel I can wait no longer and must exercise it more aggressively if I am to build up the muscle sufficiently to cope with the mountain. I pace myself cautiously and work the leg gently as I test its reactions to some road work.

However it is the practice of Zen that must be the

fundamental part of my training, and to have the greatest significance Zazen must form a substantial part of it. Zazen can be practised in either an active way or a non-active way, but there are three aspects that must be involved – the regulation of posture, the regulation of breathing and the regulation of mental activity. These three fundamentals must always be unified and combined absolutely together.

My regular physical training has to take place in the late evening, but that is quite acceptable as I like the solitude of running at night and few people are then aware of my efforts – or even of my lack of them. I live in a hilly part of London so I increase my stamina by running up a number of its long, winding roads. I also gradually build up my physical strength by wearing my back-pack, containing some of the mountain kit and equipment I will need, particularly the sleeping and bivouac bags, and every week adding a few additional items. At first I find this extremely exhausting and my determination starts to weaken, but I then prepare a mantra to force myself into even greater efforts, and slowly I toughen my resolve. I use just a simple number mantra. I count rhythmically to 100, trying to match each number to each pace, then start again, counting to another 100. Sometimes, perhaps through subconscious choice, my mind wanders and I find myself counting in the 80s, yet only remembering previously counting to the 20s. I start running some two months before the climb date, and gradually build up my nightly distance to approximately 8 miles.

As knowledge of my training schedule becomes

known to some of those who have doubted my ability to commence the climb, let alone actually complete it, more begin to accept the force of my intentions and to realise that perhaps – still only perhaps, of course – I might actually have a chance. My own fears, as I count down to the final day, sometimes increase to such an extent that I have to fight them away using all my powers of resistance. This conflict within often makes me feel I am already on Mont Blanc, already fighting to continue my climb to its Summit.

I visit a number of the climbing shops to purchase the items I need to take with me. They include a sleeping bag, a bivouac bag, an over-jacket and over-trousers, one head-torch and a variety of small items. I also purchase my own climbing boots as it has been recommended as being essential that I take with me good comfortable-fitting boots that I can rely on totally; my feet will always have to work in close harmony with my head and respond to its instructions, even when they don't want to. The other main equipment – boot crampons, ice axe, ski poles, climbing ropes – I can hire from a local mountain shop when I arrive in France. I have no thought of any subsequent climbing expeditions, and don't expect ever to need those items again. In the climbing shops in London there is a special camaraderie amongst the climbers, whether experienced or inexperienced, that I find very heartening and encouraging. Even when I explain I haven't climbed any mountains before and will actually be attempting Mont Blanc, none of them seeks to discourage me and they readily share their own experiences and recommendations with me. The only

Items Necessary For The Ascent of Mont Blanc

Clothing
Boots (Preferably well
worn-in)
Outer gloves
Inner gloves
Socks (thick and thin)
Long underwear
Trousers (or ski salopettes)
Light jacket
Windproof over-jacket
Over-trousers
Sweaters
Shirts
Hats
Gaiters

Equipment
Rucksack (back-pack)
Sleeping bag
Bivouac bag
Sleeping mat
Water bottle, cup and bowl
Kettle, stove and pot
Head-torch and spare lithium
batteries
First-aid kit
Crampons
Ice axe
Ski poles
Harness (with attached
karabiners)
Ropes and Prusik loops
Compass
Zen notebook

It is up to each individual as to the number of any of the above to be taken, plus any extra personal items (books, cameras, films, etc.), but as a mountaineer climbs, the lack of oxygen at the higher altitudes will make each item seem much heavier than its ordinary weight and become less worthwhile than it appeared at the outset. Of course, additionally, it is also necessary to carry food, water and other provisions that are vital to see a mountaineer through the rigours of the climb, particularly if any nights are to be spent sleeping out on the mountain itself (the mountain may decide this for you).

The Zen monk always sets off on his journeys carrying only his *bunko* (a box holding his *kesa* or robe), his *zagu* mat, and a strapped pair of bundles containing the rest of his entire possessions.

puzzling thing is that so many are at odds with each other with regard to their advice on the clothing and equipment I might need and the preparations I should make. But in some rather peculiar way I find this encouraging. I realise again, as in so many other areas of life, that there is never one final expert, there is no ultimate way of doing things; eventually each individual must make a personal and valued judgment after weighing up everyone else's advice and input. Zen followers use the term *karuna* to describe a process that develops slowly rather than a set quality already determined within people. I must develop further each day that passes, and each day that passes is one day nearer.

I am living the mountain daily now, so I have no need for it in my dreams. Each night's sleep is deep and sound and peaceful. My mountain mind is completely detached from the incidents and urgencies of every day and I am able to continue on two levels all the time, without either one causing the other to be less vital.

Time swirls around me as the last day approaches. I feel the mountain calling to me, and I know I will find something there that will be some kind of response or answer; perhaps an answer to a question I have not yet posed. I hope my climb will be a journey of self-knowledge. I become more eager than ever to take on the mountain's challenge and to test myself against the unknown elements I will find there.

5

JULY 1 – JOURNEY TO BASE CAMP

To reach the French chalet in Servoz, next to Chamonix, where the climbing team is to be based, I must fly to Geneva airport in Switzerland. There I will be met and taken to meet the rest of the team members. Once there my commitment must be absolute. During my own preparations I often wonder who the others are and what are their thoughts about Mont Blanc and our climbing expedition. The organisation and promotion of the climb has been through a specialist adventure club, so I assume the others are well experienced. I hope I won't hamper their own efforts and cause any of them to regret my involvement. During my nightly running I try to conjure up their physical forms, but their faces remain blank.

The morning of my flight arrives more quickly than I am prepared for. I know my training is not yet complete, but whatever is ahead I am willing to face. I wake very early but I remain some time in the bed, letting my thoughts flow in any direction they choose.

I feel myself completely attuned to the sounds of nature from outside the windows as the birds start their early morning calls to announce territorial rights. The light is strong and insistent.

After a short while I get up to shower and dress, and to push the final items inside my bulky and strained back-pack. I assume that once the team leaves the base camp we will not return, either at all or until the ascent is completed or not, so the less I take with me the less I will have to carry up the mountain. I know we intend, or expect, to bivouac on the mountain overnight and that the temperature may drop to as low as minus 30 degrees Celsius, although the wind factor can chill it to a much colder level than that. Therefore I must not leave out any items that might prove essential later on, although, of course, I will not take anything I can possibly do without.

My back-pack looks as if it has a life-force of its own; a strapped, barely contained, Quasimodo form, trying desperately to reveal itself, or perhaps to escape. It feels much heavier than I have known it in the previous few days, and I wonder if there are any further things I can leave out. But I have only included the minimum; unfortunately everything seems essential. I take out an extra battery for the head-torch, but that seems to have no effect on the overall weight, so I put it back in.

In my mountain clothes I look rather strange standing next to my solidly-built, man-made house. I feel like a foreign interloper, and am very anxious to leave. It will be at least 10 days before I can return home. Within my mind the mountain itself has now become my home; I am keen to see it, and I hope I will be welcomed.

Looking down from the aeroplane I can soon see the mountains of Europe. They look full of power and strength, and a challenge to any mountaineer. I am quietened by the thought that very soon I shall be seeing the highest, Mont Blanc, and starting out on the long ascent up its icy heights. I am the only one dressed in a climbing outfit and I look out of place amongst the well-pressed suits or dresses of the other flyers. I feel myself becoming more inward with every minute that is bringing me closer to my destination. Soon I feel as if I have lost the power of speech; I can't speak and I don't want to. I silently watch the descent of the aeroplane, the land seeming slowly to rise up to meet it. I wrap some words of Zen philosophy around me. 'Think about something three times before you say it.' My mind thinks of many things, but I do not speak at all.

At Geneva airport I wait for my back-pack to arrive on the luggage carousel. Again I look and feel very different to the other waiting passengers, mostly smartly city-dressed. I have taken with me on the aeroplane as hand-luggage one small bag containing my precious climbing boots and another one containing smaller, breakable items, in case my luggage is lost or mislaid. I had decided that the only irreplaceable items are the boots, which fit well and feel, at this stage at least, very comfortable; they are to be my companions and comforters for the hard days ahead. However I needn't have been concerned. My back-pack is the first down the luggage chute and I feel a growing excitement as I see it tumble down towards me, overturning once or twice with its own weight and bulkiness, rather than sliding down as the other cases do that follow it.

As I am still holding the other two bags with the other hand, I reach over and hoist the back-pack up with just one hand. I don't want to stop and heave it on to my back and then use its straps to even out its weight, but hold it, shoulder high, as I make my way out to the exit. It is the worst thing I could have done, a potent indication of my inexperience in preparation and technique.

The driver meeting me offers to help carry the pack or the bags, but I refuse. I want to show my self-sufficiency. He shrugs his shoulders, and is content to allow me to do my own thing. I don't feel it very much at first, but gradually as I walk a pain develops and then shoots across my right hip to my back and then to my right shoulder. The unbalanced weight from the back-pack is proving too great a strain. Still I do not lower it and re-arrange it until I am out of the terminus building. But by then, as I am later to discover more fully to my cost, the damage has been done and I have pulled or strained several muscles, particularly where my back and right hip joins.

The ride to and through Chamonix and then to the chalet is by jeep, and is long, about one-and-a-half hours. The jeep rattles and jolts me incessantly, and the pains seem to increase. In fact I know the pains have remained the same but, as Zen teaching explains, it is my awareness that is much greater, my tolerance that is much less. I concentrate on fighting away both the pain and the thought of it, and the contest is about even by the time we arrive, late in the afternoon.

I meet my fellow climbers for the first time. They look the part; wiry, lean, with muscled arms, and all of them with stories to tell of past mountaineering, ice and rock exploits. Some have even climbed to K2, one of the mightiest Himalayan mountains ranged around Mount Everest. They are younger, seem fitter and stronger, and seem considerably experienced. Still, I didn't expect anything different, and I refuse to let their obvious advantages daunt me.

I don't volunteer my injury, but in sitting down to share the evening meal it soon becomes obvious that I am in some discomfort, and I tell the others briefly about what transpired at the airport. They don't react or blame me; they all accept that injuries can happen at any time, to any climber, often in quite bizarre circumstances, and they have all suffered injuries at one time or another when climbing on previous expeditions. Such information isn't meant to be comforting, and it isn't. Mostly everyone is too wrapped up in his or her (there are two women participating) own thoughts and preparations to worry about me, and they don't sympathise with my bad luck.

It starts to come home to me how solitary an endeavour climbing really is, even subsequently, when roped one to another. At all times an individual must make his or her own decisions and judgments. No one can climb for you; no one can decide whether you are fit to climb or to continue; no one but yourself can make that ascent to the Summit. There is an intensity of mood and feeling that precludes conversation and comment, and most faces appear strained in anticipation of what tomorrow may bring.

The chalet becomes totally silent as we retreat to our individual rooms to check through our equipment and make our final preparations. We are sleeping two to a room, but apart from the perfunctory polite words of greeting and goodnight no discussions or involved conversations take place that night. I feel there are many ghosts listening and prowling around, and the mountain at times seems to be inside the chalet, straining to get at us, as if we are the ones waiting to be conquered.

6

JULY 2 – PAINS AND PREPARATIONS

The first part of the night I lie on my bed trying to sleep. I attempt to ignore the pains in my back and hip, but they drive away any chance of sleep. I hear the steady breathing of my companion in the other bed and presume he is asleep. I do not want to disturb him, so, after some time of uncomfortably turning to one side, then to the other, probably after midnight, I rise as quietly as I can and step outside the room to the annexe section built over the main stairs, and lie down on the wooden floor to try to rest there. I know I will not sleep now, so I allow my mind to roam freely and to explore its own possibilities without being too aware of my body, which still keeps trying to speak. I try to use my awakened state to prepare myself for the morning and what lies ahead. If my body will be less rested than those of the other climbers, at least I hope my mind can be better prepared.

Wryly I remember the Zen principle that a person is already awakened and it's only necessary to become aware of this. Zen always hopes to point the way from bondage to freedom. Following Zen is a way of awakening. There is no difference between an enlightened person and an ignorant one, other than the fact that one realises he is awake whilst the other still has to gain that realisation. In a Zen way, the pains I am experiencing are heightening my awareness and my thoughts of the mountain. I can't see it in the darkness; but I can see it in the light within.

One of the great Zen sayings is that nothing is possible without three essential elements: a great root of faith, a great ball of doubt and fierce tenacity of purpose. I feel that these three elements are with me at all times. I expect to succeed; although I am constantly racked with doubts, I hope I will fight to the end to achieve my goal.

I try to accept the pain as an additional force that will help me to achieve my objectives. I remain conscious of my body and I know it will have an equal part to play if I am to obtain the success I seek. Some words of Zen Master Omori Sogen Rotaishi echo through the darkened chalet and fill the night. 'Zen without realisation of the body is empty speculation.' I am beginning at last to understand what he meant. I get up, and stand and sit in different positions throughout the chalet. I can hear the rhythmic breathing of the others, all of whom seem to be sleeping peacefully and easily. It feels as if the whole world is sleeping and I am the only one awake.

I open the door of the chalet and step out on to the veranda, with its stairs at one end leading to the gardens and pathways below. The night is completely still, not the slightest hint of wind or of any sound apart from those I make myself. There is some light but I can see no more than 10 metres in any direction before the sights blur into nothingness. I know where Mont Blanc is and stare at it without seeing it, yet always seeing it.

As I have not slept, I am first up in the morning, the others slowly joining me, by which time I have set out the breakfast for everyone. Politeness is the order of the day as we gently probe each other's capabilities and reasons for being there. Everyone is reticent, no one too intrusive; we respect each other's reserve. It is easier to talk about unimportant things.

Kit and equipment inspection is next. No two people's back-packs are similar. When everything is removed and all is spread out on the grass verges outside the chalet, it looks like a bring and buy sale of odd clothing and items. Very few have all the equipment needed for the mountains, so it is necessary to make a trip into Chamonix to hire the additional items needed. It means a delay before we commence the first day's climbing, but I am very pleased as it gives me a few extra hours for my back pains to ease, and time for me to start to recover. I need that time.

In fact everyone else seems just as keen to hold back and visit Chamonix. It is a small village, and practically all those living or working there are involved with the mountains, either preparing for climbing or assisting those who want to climb. I hire an ice axe, two ski poles, and crampons that are adjusted to fit my climbing boots. The crampons are two iron frames that lock around the boots, leaving 10 protruding spikes that are to grip into the ice or the rock as the circumstances dictate. They look, and are, a vicious and fierce apparatus, transforming the feet into combative aggressors.

The other team members also finalise their own crampon and other equipment hire. There is some frantic last minute re-arrangements as everyone realises that this is the last chance to change anything. After today whatever we have is what we must use to help us climb the mountain. And that goes just as much for our mental equipment; it's our time for the mountains. I am yet more conscious of the aches I feel in my back and hip, and quickly purchase some recommended ointment from the pharmacy, then slip away to find a secluded doorway, undo my clothing and rub the ointment as far as I can reach. It soothes immediately and feels effective and promising.

Everyone is already crammed inside the jeep as I place my pack and equipment on top of theirs, piled haphazardly in the rear, and then clamber on and squeeze myself aboard. We are driven out of Chamonix and through the outskirts to reach a long, winding, exceedingly bumpy, track. This in turn takes us to a steep grassy area that we must climb in order to reach the higher, wooded slopes that encircle the approaches to Mont Blanc, guarded as it is by its ring of soldier mountains.

7

THE WAY OF THE MOUNTAIN

It is the Way of the mountain, the Way of Mont Blanc. The Japanese affix the suffix *do* to the names of Zen arts. *Do* usually translates as the Way, the equivalent perhaps of the Chinese *tao*. *Kendo* is the Way of the sword or the spear; *kyudo* is the Way of the bow; *aikido* is the Way of harmony with *ki*, the driving force of the universe. But there is no word in common use for the Way of the mountain. *Tozan* is Japanese for mountain-eering and *noboru* for climbing, but neither *tozando* nor *noborudo* has the right feel or sound to me. Japanese is a rich language, and both *yama* or *san* can be used to mean mountain (although *san* is not used on its own); so it's possible to use *Fujiyama* or *Fujisan* to mean Mount Fuji. I decide to create a new word, *sando*, as meaning the Way of the mountain, leading me to the Way of Mont Blanc. I bow towards the mountain, and whisper *sando* to the wind, hoping it will carry all the way to the Summit.

The weather seems good, but we can see Mont

Blanc only intermittently through the white cumulus clouds that roll across the skyline. The mountain appears a long way off and I try not to think about it too deeply, as I know it will be some days before the final challenge will be issued and eventually accepted. We start climbing up through the woods between les Bossons, and then follow a steep but manageable rocky path that should eventually lead us above the rocks and on to the lower Glaciers des Bossons.

Our pace is fast, and at first I find it difficult to match the speed of the others. I tussle within to try and find an acceptable rhythm that will enable me to keep up with them without over-exerting myself, but that will not cause me to become too exhausted at this early stage. The back-pack feels heavier than I expected; I am too aware of it, and try mentally to free myself from its pressure. I concentrate again on the three fundamentals of Zazen. I know that if I can control and balance these three, together they will combine and allow me to experience a special state of mind, and I might then enter the realm of Zen awareness.

The first way is the regulation of posture. I straighten my body, ground my legs and steps and feel myself secured to the land underneath.

Next I concentrate on my breathing, keeping it steady, firm and equal. In Zen it is impossible to overstate the importance of breathing. In knowing and using Zen it is vital to breathe from the lower abdomen – the *hara* – that part of the abdomen below the navel. *Tanden* is not only the centre of *hara*, about 5 centimetres below the navel, but is also taken to be the centre of a person, both physically and psychologically. Physically *tanden* is a person's centre of gravity; psychologically *tanden* is the centre of the personality. If it is said that a person has *hara*, it means that that person is considered to be well balanced and secure, both physically and psychologically. *Hara* is a way of lowering the centre of gravity so that a person can withstand greater pressures and forces; that is one reason why a *sumo* wrestler concentrates on his bulk and his stomach, and fights with his abdomen as a positive weapon of opposition to his opponents. But *hara* also means being balanced emotionally; a person with *hara* is less likely to react badly or foolishly; they will have a sense of courage, the strength to face adversity and a strong capacity for endurance. All the way up I struggle for my *hara* to continue with me. I feel I have won.

The third but equally important Zen fundamental is concentration. Only with total strength of concentration can one make certain that one's stance, posture and breathing follow the Way. Within the use of concentration, *susoku* means counting the breathing. Each exhalation is one breath. It is accepted that *susoku* is a counting to 10, started over again and again. If I am counting to 100, as I am now on the mountain and as I had when I attempted it in my nightly running, this can be taken as 10 of 10 in the practice of *susoku*.

I am so engrossed in these fundamentals that time itself has no meaning. Soon I find myself easily keeping up with the others, almost without effort. I do not need to rest any longer, and even when they stop I remain standing, waiting till they recommence. We stop twice and, although not thirsty, each time I drink some water, in case I need it without my realising it.

Somehow we have climbed too far and are some distance above the glacier line. I step warily to the cliff edge and look at its steep, boulder-strewn slopes. At the bottom is the glacier path we need. Possibly we will have to retrace our steps until we find the path we have missed. But there is another way down. And so the decision is made. Not collectively. Perhaps too nonchalantly. We are to abseil down the rock-face to reach the pathway leading to the glaciers.

8

FIRST ABSEIL

The thought of abseiling down a long, steep, rocky cliff-face will be daunting, even to anyone who has abseiled before. To someone like myself, who has never abseiled, the thought, soon to be brought to reality, is awesome. The faces of the other climbers remain completely impassive, and I do not reveal my fears to them.

Learning Zen is unlearning, and I know that this will be one of the keys to my abseiling the rock success-fully. But learning Zen is also part of the process of challenging previous concepts I have held, of striving to master them yet being always aware of possible defeat. Zen is a way of leaning inwards and leaning outwards at the same time, of using seemingly contra-dictory principles to advance oneself, mentally and physically. *Samsara* is the circle of self-frustrating effort, and it is essential to break out of this circle in order to obtain achievement, while at all times being awake to all possibilities. This is the fundamental basis of *satori*

Zen. I am almost ready to go for it.

Niwazume is the period of endurance and tests set for Zen novices wanting to learn and to be taught Zen, who are kept waiting until it is decided they are really ready for teaching. *Niwazume* can continue for days, sometimes months, and may never end if it is felt that the individual is still not ready in attitude and spirit to step forward to the beginning. I constantly feel as if I am having to undertake *niwazume* – continually preparing myself for the final Mont Blanc ascent. Yet I know I shouldn't express any doubts, otherwise the mountain will probably frustrate me.

I am anxious to take the test now, to volunteer to go before my courage starts to waver. My nerves are very taut. I hope the rope will be as taut once I start to lower myself down. I ask only one question – 'Do I jump from rock to rock in a continuing movement?'

'Not if you don't want to break your legs' is the casual, discouraging response. 'You can only do that against a flat wall or surface. Here you must work your way down slowly, bending the knees, to find a firm base with one leg before searching for another hold with the other leg. Good luck, and don't stop or you may freeze, and no one wants to have to go down after you to take you down.'

A rope is loosely looped around a tree and then in turn looped around my waist and joined to a karabiner hook that is fastened to my strapped waist harness. First of all I face the nothingness beyond the cliff, then deliberately stand on its very edge and look downwards. The whole way down is littered with rocks and stones of differing sizes. It looks hazardous, almost

[*37*]

unclimbable. The drop is sheer and it seems a very long way to the bottom.

I turn and face my judges. I am conscious of some pain in my back, but it quickly transfers to my brain as that takes control of the next few, very long, moments. I step backwards off the edge, and for one lengthy second my lead foot touches nothing. My weight obeys the laws of gravity. It is a moment before oblivion. I concentrate my total forces, reaching out with my feet for the rocks somewhere below me. One foot connects, grips firmly to the rock-face, then I move downwards again, letting go, feeling myself falling free. Each second seems to last an eternity, only to end as I am rewarded with something solid that arrests my descent.

I disappear below the rim and lose sight of everything except the rock wall immediately in front of me. It has texture, form and life; it holds my life to it. I must think only of the moment. Everything is transient, always changing, never constant. I must remain alert and respond instantly to the slightest movement in rope and rock, to the very air itself. I concentrate on my breathing, and it steadies me. I continue downwards, slowly, letting out the rope gradually, hoping that the person guiding and following the rope on the cliff top will be able to hold it firmly if I should lose my foothold and start to slide and perhaps tumble downwards. At times it seems only the strength of my arms is preventing me from falling. My boots thud strongly against the rocks with each further step downwards.

Eventually, probably much later – I have lost my judgment of time, as I would do on many subsequent occasions – I realise I am not going to fall, that I will make it to the bottom. At that moment my foot dislodges a stone, and there is nothing to hold me. I feel myself start to slip, and am about to lose control. I fight with myself and with the rocks, trying to maintain my balance and position. The contest seems unequal. I dare not fail as I am certain it will affect the rest of my subsequent efforts, and might even destroy my fragile determination to climb the glaciers and rocks on the way to the Summit. My feet scramble in mid-air and I hang heavily on the rope, which threatens to pull me away from the rock face. Then both feet make contact. I brace them hard, and am in control again. From that moment on I do not treat the mountain with anything but the greatest respect, and do not relax again until I am safely down.

Finally I free the rope and watch it snake back up the cliff, to bring the next climber down. I then use my ice axe to balance me on my way down the lower and easier slopes. At the bottom, next to the path leading to the first glacier, I wait for the others to join me. I have gained control of myself. So far. But there is still a long way to go.

9

FIRST GLACIER

Glaciers are things of absolute and sheer beauty. They appear at first remote and aloof, but in fact give out an inviting warmth that would seem to be capable of melting anyone or anything – except another glacier. They appear to be smooth, but often are not; they look soft, but are rock hard and make no concessions. They bar the way like guardians of the mountain; you must either climb them or stay below. On behalf of the mountain they ask the question 'Who are you?' If you cannot answer immediately they will wait, for eventually you will respond, you will answer.

It is time to put on my boot crampons. Without the use of crampons, attempting the smallest icy slope can turn into an epic of frustrating efforts. When I clip and strap them to the boots I feel and become a different person, at least for the initial approach to, and attack on, the first glacier. The fierce sharp-edge harsh 10 points, spaced around the metal frame, are to grip me to the ice when I walk or climb the mountain, and are to take my full weight even when balancing and leaning out from it. They look cruel and mediaeval, and have to be used cruelly if I am to survive. Possibly it's like the moment when it's decided between a horse and its rider who is to be in control, who is to be the master. However that's where the great danger lies. For the mountain is always the master and always ends up in control. I am here just as a guest, whether invited or uninvited. At any time I can be made to leave, and if I refuse to go I may never be able to leave.

Ji refers to the technical aspects of a Zen art. *Ri* is the underlying principles of the universe, the universal truths, formless and unchanging. *Ri* denotes inspiration, whereas *ji* denotes skill. Now I will have to concentrate on the *ji* of the crampon.

When using the crampons, and particularly when descending, it is important to bend the knees, putting the full weight on to the boots, through them on to the crampons, then pressing fully through to the mountain below the ice. When climbing in crampons you usually walk in a zigzag fashion in order to ascend with the minimum of effort, although if you feel strong enough you can walk in a straight line. I try it sometimes, but my knees will not easily forgive me. In contrast, you should always descend in a straight line, leaning down the slope, knees bent to lock into the mountain, but it takes a great deal of courage to do this when there seems to be nothing to prevent you from falling headfirst downwards. The descent technique is learned slowly, but in order to progress I must trust only in myself and be prepared to lean forwards, seemingly supported on the air itself. The first time is a very telling moment; nothing exists around and within me as I battle with gravity, trying to confound it.

This is my glacier. Someone has to climb first, but whoever does so must climb alone, unaided, without ropes. It is a hard, private decision, for one must rely on personal skills, method and speed. For those that climb second or after, the challenge of the glacier wall remains but they will at least then have the help of a safety rope. I have never climbed ice before. Only that day had I worn crampons for the first time, and I am still hesitant about their use. Abseiling has been a test of climbing down; now I am to undergo a test of climbing upwards. Is it beyond my capabilities? I will soon know. Zen teaches you never to accept a limit without testing to and beyond that limit, and that's how this moment feels.

I am to climb next. I lay down my large ice axe and am handed two small ice axes. The guide rope is tied to my waist harness, and I am again nonchalantly waved forward. Approaching the glacier wall I become the loneliest man in this world of snow and ice. I have no real concept of what it will feel like and how I will manage the ascent. It looks terrifying, and of course it is. The wall is sheer ice, perhaps 30 metres in height. It gives no quarter, and time waits impatiently for my decision: whether I'll proceed or back away.

In each Zen art there are usually many techniques to master but in *kyudo*, the way of the bow, there are only eight. These steps or stages are called *hassetu*, and there are three stages in *hassetu* that I treat as particularly relevant to this glacier challenge. Stage six is known as *kai*, the meeting. I touch the base of the wall and, through my glove, I feel its hardness and unyielding force. I have met the glacier and I accept its awesome potency. Stage one of *hassetu* is *ashihumi*, meaning to step or tread; it is always the first physical move to make, and now it is mine. I raise one hand above my head and strike an ice axe into the ice as high as I can reach. It holds firmly, so I do the same with the other. I am now at full stretch, pressed closely against the wall, my eyes a few millimetres away from it. There is nothing else that exists, only the ice wall and myself. I raise one leg and kick the boot and its crampon hard into the wall. The spikes pierce the ice and hold. I lift my other leg off the ground, my total weight now held by the two ice axes and the one crampon, and again kick into the wall. It also holds. I am now stretched flat against the wall, perhaps half a metre off the ice floor below. I pull out one ice axe, stretch upwards and again strike it firmly into the ice above. I follow with the second ice axe, then with the crampons, and quickly repeat the actions several times before I pause to gather some further strength.

I look down. I am now some 5 or 6 metres off the ground. I hug myself to the glacier, totally reliant upon the ice axes and crampons holding me firmly and preventing my falling backwards and downwards. I am gasping with the exertions I have made, and try to control my breathing and to concentrate on the task that still lies ahead. It is extremely difficult and I am totally aware of the anxious thoughts of those watching me from below. I can sense their own fears of their climbs that are to follow mine, and I feel very vulnerable. I become conscious that my arms and legs are

[*43*]

becoming tired and that there is a long way still to climb. I question whether my limbs have the strength to continue. I fight hard to eliminate the doubts that are insistently pushing themselves into my consciousness. I know the longer I wait the more tired my arms and legs will become, supporting, as they are, my entire weight. Mentally I push away everything else and only think of my next action.

I pull out one ice axe too vigorously, and in so doing I feel my weight following it. I am moving away from the glacier into space and into nothingness. Everything slows around me as I struggle to regain my balance and try to lean again into the glacier. Whilst still not certain it will work, I swing my hand in a half-circle and back into the glacier wall. The axe pierces its skin and it holds. The effort of the struggle will probably not have been seen by those watching below; to them time will have moved at its normal, ordinary pace. Only to me does so much time seemed to have passed, and so many fears to have presented themselves: the fear of the mountain itself, the fear of failure, the fear of pain, the fear of having to try again, the fear of losing strength – and the absolute blackness of fear itself.

Gently I pull my left boot away from the ice, move my leg upwards and kick the crampons in. Will they hold? A flurry of snow and ice fall from the wall, as if to confirm my doubts. There is no way back. I pull out the right ice axe, even less vigorously this time, and pause momentarily to decide where best to aim it. I strike it in firmly, and once more am spreadeagled against the wall, wondering. How many times will I have to repeat this process before I reach the glacier rim? Will it continue to be successful each time? Will it ever become any easier?

It never does. I never once feel at ease. Throughout the climb I am continually tensed in anticipation of the dangers. There are so many chances of mishap, and each action creates those chances yet again. Sometimes the blow of my ice axe is not strong enough to penetrate the wall. Yet if I swing the axe too hard, the action threatens to unbalance me. Also, if the axe strikes too hard and penetrates too deeply, it takes a greater effort to release it, and that in turn could cause me to swing out from the mountain. Furthermore, the spikes of the crampons are only a few centimetres long, and I can feel them working themselves loose; they have no ratchet to catch on, and the thin metal works only as a downward support provided I am leaning well into the wall, but it is so difficult to do this when I am trying to move upwards. My weight is mostly being supported by my arms hanging on to the ice axes, but they are tiring rapidly from their efforts of holding me into the wall, then of pulling one axe out and striking it in above my head. Fiercely I thrust away any thoughts of my becoming too tired to continue, but they rebound equally fiercely and hang around me, weighting me downwards.

Although it is perhaps the wrong thing to do, I quicken my pace. Not pausing to wait any further, I start pulling out and swinging the second ice axe the moment the other has struck and has seemed to have held. I look up, and the rim seems far away. I look again, and now I am just below it. I realise I am going to make it, and then I hardly feel the weight of my feet as my arms move me upwards and over the glacier's edge. I stand on top of it and look down at the others, so far below, and I feel marvellous. Stage seven of *hassetu* is *hanare*, the release, and I release myself into the warmth of the ice that seems finally to invite me. After *hanare* all tension is at an end.

The margin between success and failure, even disaster, on the mountain, is very small. Up to now I've had success, although it never really feels that way; it always seems as if it could so easily go the other way. But now, for the first time, I am to experience failure, and in doing so I learn even greater respect for the mountain.

After all the team have completed their practise climbs up several glacier faces we are all to return to base camp by making our way down a route that will take us directly back to the valley floor. We walk in a straight line where we can, and use our large ice axes and the ski poles to support us down the steeper and more complex sections. But eventually we arrive at a downward-sloping ice gully, narrower at the bottom than the top, that completely bars our way. We can return and look for an easier route, perhaps by taking a longer way around and down, but we decide not to refuse the challenge. In Zen the wrong way to do something is known as *muri*, but often you will not know it is the wrong way until you have tried and failed. It is not a contradiction, but an extension of the thought of *muri*, that Zen is letting go and believing, even if in letting go you actually fail. Trying to force change or a different approach on a person is like *muri*. It's better, it's the right way, to look for the line, the point, of least resistance. Yet – and again it is no contradiction – Zen accepts that there are two or more ways; the now depends upon a standpoint that may change with your perspective of a situation or a person.

As I can't reach both sides of the upper gully, my choice, my decision, is to straddle the lower part, one foot positioned on either side, my crampons gripping tightly to each bank, using my ski poles to balance and to propel me forwards. I manage the first few steps, after which point there is no going back. Words of encouragement and instructions are shouted to me, but I can't readily comprehend them, and certainly can't convert them into instructions to my feet. I have reached the possibility of too many choices, the if point, an impossible position, where to lift either leg will leave me partly unsupported and unbalanced, and in danger of free-fall. The moment lengthens and I can hear nothing except my own thoughts within my brain, working through the possibilities, until gradually they exhaust themselves and also fall silent. I know I cannot move without falling, and it becomes an exercise in limitation. How am I to fall without causing too much harm to myself, perhaps damaging myself seriously and thus finishing any chance I might have of completing the Summit climb, and without possibly endangering the others who have to follow me?

I have to let go and believe. I lift one leg into the air and lean my total weight on the other, pushing into the ice with a ski pole, slowly trying to propel myself forwards and then trying to slide the other leg downwards. Crampons do not slide, and I topple over, slowly, falling into the bottom of the gully that eagerly welcomes me. I try not to pierce myself with any of the crampon spikes and pole points, although harsh metal seems to be surrounding me. The blood loss is small, and the red drops on the white ice make me think of Snow White.

There is no comment or sound from the others, but I feel their sympathy and understanding. Am I now experiencing the sound of one hand clapping, perhaps the most well known of Hakuin's Zen *koans*? Despite the defeat and the pain it is a sudden, joyous, inner explosion to feel that, perhaps, I have experienced an enlightenment of a sort. The knowledge helps me to right myself, to lever myself out of the gully, to clamber to the end and safety. Unfortunately I have set a pattern for most of the others who have to follow, and one by one they also tumble down the gully, only two of the team managing to remain upright and to reach the bottom safely. I feel I have been bloodied, in the way a novice at a sport often is in order to learn and respect the way that the sport is played.

I am silent all the rest of the climb down on our way back to the base camp. In many ways the incident helps me to have less fear and to relax more. Another Zen saying comes to mind and seems particularly important. 'It is important to live rather than define.' With the fall I have also realised just how far there is to go, how much there is to accomplish, and just how many chances of failure there are. The Summit is still very far off. So many of those who have attempted to climb the mountain before me have not managed to reach it, but to the mountain it matters not at all. I am no longer certain how much it still matters to me. Is it the fatigue speaking or an inner voice of knowledge? I decide that neither the subject nor the time are appropriate for this sort of mental tussle.

At the chalet it is time for hot showers, food and some reflection. The rain, intermittent over the last few hours, is now falling steadily. It seems a worrying omen and helps to isolate us. I learn that the intention is in fact to return to the chalet after each day's climbing, gradually extending the height of our ascents over the next three or four days, and hopefully creating the necessary acclimatisation within each of us. This will prepare us for the rigorous final few days when it's expected we will climb all the way to the Summit in two or three stages. The weather is so unpredictable that it's important to try and have one day in hand in case we are beaten back and need to try again. I realise now I should have brought with me some extra clothes and more books, and kept them at the base camp. I will just content myself with interchanging my jerseys and shirts in different sequences of wear. I take out my Zen notebook, protected by its waterproof cover, and spend most of the evening trying to capture within it the emotions and images conjured up by the moods and feelings of the mountain. Whilst climbing I always keep the notebook inside an inner pocket of my overjacket; it's the most precious object I carry with me, and I mustn't take the chance of losing it.

10

JULY 3 – LEARNING ROPE

The atmosphere in the chalet is relaxed, and the evening meal is being prepared amidst a bustle of light-hearted banter and playful joshing, particularly between those who have climbed together on previous expeditions. There is ample time to clean our kit and equipment in preparation for the next day's climbing. I have brought the least of anyone, but I have not worn some of the extra sweaters that I'll need on the higher snow ridges, so I put one on. Everyone puts on something bright and cheerful, so that the clothes match our mood.

We have accomplished something really worthwhile today, both in tackling the abseil descent and climbing the glacier, and we all made it. I am pleased I held my own with the others and matched their pace and standards. The expedition leader decides to organise us into two sets of six, and I feel fortunate he includes me in his group. The other is led by another very experienced climber, a long-standing friend of his, and most of the evening they exchange tales of past exploits and adventures, each of them trying to outdo the other. All the stories emphasise the dangers of mountain climbing and how close each has nearly come to disaster. I cannot make up my mind whether they are trying to discourage us or are just alerting us to the necessity of constantly being aware of how important it is to take extreme care at all times. I am impressed by their knowledge and experience, and I try not to reveal my own inadequacies and lack of mountaineering background. Within the 12 climbers I am the oldest; some are still at university, but no one seems interested in that or prepared to judge anyone else. We are very much aware there are still some six or seven days ahead before the final assault on the Summit, and a lot can happen in that time. No one knows who may or may not make it to the top, or who may have to be left behind, although I guess that the two team leaders have their private opinions. The thought makes me feel a little nervous, but I do not try to express my concerns, and instead excuse myself from the table.

As it has stopped raining I step outside the chalet door to be welcomed by the warm, though wet, night air. It's very cloudy and I can see neither stars nor moon. I know where Mont Blanc is, but it cannot be seen. Even on a bright day, when it is clear everywhere else, the mountain is usually cloaked in some cloud, almost always partly hidden, as if hoping to dissuade those who are determined to try and climb it. I can hear the noisy sounds of chatter and laughter from within, in stark contrast to the deep stillness outside. There's not a sound out here – not a bird, not a bat, not even any wind. I feel myself to be a conduit through which the noise and the quietness are both trying to pass, one tussling with the other. Not surprisingly the quietness wins; gradually the sounds die away and vanish, or perhaps I choose not to hear them. I try to ready my state of mind for the challenges ahead. Everything I need is within me, if only I can reach into it. The words of Zen Master Dashu say it all: 'The treasure house within you contains everything, and you are free to use it. You don't need to seek outside.'

It is a bad and stressful night for me. Lying on my back seems to aggravate the strains. I try turning on to each side, then on to my front, but nothing seems to alleviate the pain, no position is any more satisfactory than another. Eventually, when I judge everyone is asleep, as on the previous night, I quietly leave my room and my sleeping companion and take up a sitting position on the downstairs wooden floor. I try to calm myself spiritually and mentally to compensate for the lack of physical rest. The night passes slowly. I can only hope time is on my side. I use more of the ointment and it helps a little. The rain is again beating down outside and I concentrate on the rhythmic sound. It is hypnotically relaxing, and I do sleep in fitful patches. I dream of the oceans; I try to include the mountains, but they refuse to appear and the oceans are completely black and without any end.

Naturally I am first up again. I quickly shower and start to prepare breakfast. It is still raining, and we learn that the weather forecast is bad and unlikely to improve. Although it is an accepted and often normal situation in climbing, and I know it would be foolish and dangerous to start in these conditions, it is still very frustrating. We have only a few days to spare, so it will mean that we will have less time to acclimatise slowly, which may be a problem for the less experienced climbers. Although that means me in particular, I refuse to allow the thought to faze me as there are too many other concerns I must also contend with. I am realising more and more how tough a venture this is and that the prospects of success are not favourable. In order not to waste the time too much, and as the rain has finally slowed to a drizzle, we assemble in the open to undergo rope and knot-tying practice.

It is always possible that any one of us might become separated from the others in the course of the ascent or the descent, and it is important to know certain basic rope techniques for use in an emergency. Knots are the link connecting the climber to the rope and, via this, to the rock and to the ice. An ability to recognise and use a variety of knots in different circumstances can be vital, the difference between disaster and success on the mountain. A knot therefore needs to be neatly tied, small, above all strong, and hopefully incapable of coming undone except by choice. Each knot has its own name and particular use and purpose. I haven't thought about or used knots since childhood, and it takes a little while before I start to have some feel for them.

The simplest knot of all is the overhand knot, also known as the thumb knot, whereby the rope is just turned in upon itself; it is often used as a stopper knot to secure a rope end that itself has another knot tied in it. The fisherman's knot is used for joining two rope-ends together. It is really two overhand knots, each tied round the other rope and pulled tightly together; as with so many other knots, they can themselves be doubled, and then are particularly useful in joining ropes together extremely securely and firmly. The figure-of-eight looks as it sounds; it is the basic and the most versatile climbing knot, very useful for forming loops for support or loading; it is easy to tie, very strong, yet easy to untie in a hurry. Then there are knots with wonderful and descriptive names – alpine butterfly, lark's foot, clove hitch, and many more – but I have to content myself with trying to learn only the original three. Even so I have great difficulties in remembering and mastering the intricacies of the Way of the Rope.

In order to be roped one to another when climbing the mountain, each person must wear one of the many kinds of support harnesses. A thigh-loop harness is preferred, to cope with harsh and difficult rock and ice routes, and this is what I have. The harness loops around the waist and thighs, and is then knotted to remain secure at all times. It takes a little getting used to, but is absolutely essential. The joining ropes are then attached to the harness by a karabiner, usually of the screw-gate type; this is a metal buckle that can be quickly screwed tight or loosened, but that should not come undone accidentally. If a climber slips, then often the only thing that will save him from falling down the mountain is the combined strength of his harness and the karabiner. It may be some time before the others to whom he is roped are able to pull him to safety, so his total weight, and possibly that of his back-

Ice axing up the glacier wall.

Crampon practice on the lower ice slopes.

Fighting through the blizzard across the Aiguille.

The slow climb continues.

At Tête Rousse.

Looking back in awe.

The silence reaches out.

Arriving at the Refuge du Goûter.

Relaxing and gathering resolve.

Waiting for the weather at the peak to improve.

Enjoying the solitude.

High above the clouds.

The final ascent in pitch darkness (3 a.m.).

The final steps onto the summit ridge.

Presenting the Children's Charity flag at the Summit.

The last moments at 15,771 feet on the Mont Blanc summit.

The descent view.

pack and equipment, will be relying on the strength of his safety apparatus. Karabiners have the locking screw at the side, so are strongest along their length. It has been known for karabiners to open under stress and too heavy a weight, but even so, if the mountaineer stays calm, it is still possible for the others to pull him slowly to safety if the knots are well tied and the ropes are not allowed to slacken, allowing the karabiner to slip sideways.

The rain has stopped, but it's too late to make a start today, so we hope to start off early the next morning. It means we can spend some more time practising our knots, and also learn some rope-climbing techniques. The chalet has several protruding beams near the roof, and a rope is secured to one and dropped all the way to the ground. The idea is to climb this rope unaided, weighed down with one's back-pack.

It is explained that it's always necessary to be prepared for any kind of emergency or accident on the mountain. The climber may fall and injure himself, and the others (maybe there is only one other) may not be able to reach him. Although he may want to lessen his weight by jettisoning his back-pack, this may subsequently prove to be extremely foolhardy, particularly if he has to bivouac (sleep out) on the mountain overnight before he can return to safety. Or the climber may slip down a crevasse, perhaps 3 metres or more below the surface, where there may be no room for him to use his crampons or ice-axe (if he still has it) to climb out.

In these and other cases the only solution may be for the climber to ascend the rope by using an ascending knot technique called the Prusik knot method, named after an Austrian climber, Dr Karl Prusik. The principle works on the basis of looping one smaller rope tightly around the main support rope so that it grips and fixes to it when loaded and bearing weight. The climber sometimes loops two Prusik knots around the climbing rope, puts his weight on the lower loop and slides the other loop up to a point he can reach with one foot. He then transfers his weight to the higher of the two loops and releases the lower one, removing it and looping up to a point where his other foot can reach. He continues this process until he reaches the safety of the rim or ledge. Even if he is injured and can only use one leg, there is a single Prusik loop technique that can be used. The weight is temporarily taken off the sound leg by the arms, and the leg is used to slide the loop up the climbing rope. The sound leg is then straightened while standing in the loop, and the procedure repeated. It is a slow method, but it can save a climber's life.

This single Prusik loop method is the one we are to try, using our fisherman's knots to tie it to the climbing rope. I watch till the last person has somehow scrambled up, as it's suggested I do not try to climb this way in case I place too great a strain on my back and cause it to give way – it's too risky to chance that at this stage. My reason agrees, but my heart refuses to back away; I do not want to be the only one of the team not to have attempted to try this technique and challenge. Some climbers before me had found it very unnerving, so I feel there's a lot of sympathy for me as I step forward to the rope. I tie on my Prusik loop, slide it up, and it secures itself. I place my right foot in it, about waist high and push upwards. Amazingly it all goes according to plan and I am suddenly a metre off the ground. I lean backward into the air, loosen my weight and slide the Prusik higher. My right foot is now above my head. I heave myself upwards and I am standing upright, my weight held by the Prusik, so that I am now about 2 metres off the ground. I can do it. It is a great strain, but at all times I'm particularly conscious of my back, wondering if I will hear a sudden crack and feel a pain come shooting through it. Fortunately my back holds, and soon I've clambered over the chalet balcony and to safety. It is a good feeling to have accomplished this small rope climb.

The rest of the day we are allowed to do anything we choose to, and most of us walk down to the village store to stock up on provisions for the next two days at least. We are expecting to climb to the high ice ridges early the next morning in an endeavour to reach Mont Tacul; we will probably spend at least one night out on the mountain there, and everything we need we must take with us. I hope we can avoid the crevasses so that I won't need to use the rope techniques that I've barely mastered.

Surprisingly my back is feeling a great deal easier. Perhaps the rope climbing stretched the muscles. For the first time I sleep through most of the night. I am still the first to wake up, but take much longer over my shower; it may be the last for some days. I am pleased to find breakfast waiting for me when I've dressed.

11

JULY 4 – ASCEND THE NEEDLE, ACROSS TO THE TACUL

I know the mountain is waiting for me. I think I am ready for it. As ready as I'll ever be. Today is to be a major test for our altitude responses. We decide we will journey up to the top of the Aiguille du Midi – very high, at 3,842 metres – and climb across at that height. To confront a mountain at that altitude takes great care and it will be a serious challenge to the determination and conditioning of all of us.

In order to travel to that height quickly we use the *téléphérique* cable cars. The *téléphérique* saves climbers a great deal of time, but it does disfigure the mountain. I do not voice my distaste to the others, so as not to dampen their spirits, but I hope that no more cable-car routes are built, and that the mountain is left to itself. It is a great natural force and it must be protected against misuse. A climber challenges, ascends, then descends, and the mountain is left again in peace. A man-made cable system is permanent; it disturbs nature and the *shin* of the mountain. As if answering my thoughts, the mountain confirms its power. At the next cable stop, Piton Central, as we are changing to a higher section, I see a number of people being brought down, crying from the effects of the lack of oxygen. They are disorientated, suffering from severe mental pressure and the pain from trying to breathe in the much thinner atmosphere. Everyone falls silent at seeing their predicament; inwardly we sympathise, but we must all steel ourselves to proceed upwards.

We soon reach the top level of the Aiguille station, 3,842 metres, step out on to the exposed side of the mountain and proceed to fasten on our crampons. The wind is terribly fierce and we are quickly frozen by its bitterness. The way to proceed is to cross a very narrow ice ridge, but to reach that ridge we first have to edge slowly around a corner bluff, with a path less than half a metre wide. It looks, and is, highly dangerous, and we rope into our two teams of six to traverse it. There is one particularly nerve-wracking moment when I am finely balanced, leaning into the unyielding, slippery ice wall, with nothing to hold on to; only able to stay upright and oppose the hypnotic pull from the icy wastes below by steadying my mind to think and to edge myself forward and across. It is one of my longest moments on the mountain. I am pleased when I overcome it, but I will not be keen to submit to that test again; it requires my practice of *samadhi*, the Zen process of intense concentration, and the strain is immense.

In Zen, random thoughts from lack of concentration

are called delusions, and in this fierce and bitter atmosphere I must constantly fight against the demons that threaten to delude me into taking a false step. Zen teaches that each action, each step, each decision, is final and decisive, just as each moment is the ultimate one at the time it occurs. Time can never be recaptured, it is unique. Once a moment has gone it cannot be repeated. Too many people seek to repeat a special moment instead of moving on. But in Zen it is understood there are no second times, no real second chances. One must put every effort into paying the fullest attention to each instant of life, to every action and activity, no matter how trivial it may seem. Each action should be undertaken as if it is the only activity on Earth. For all of us, at that precise moment, it is.

We hike down the lengthy and barren ice ridge underneath the south face, and cross to the right of Gros Rognon and la Tour Ronde so that we can camp on the plateau of Mont Tacul. Its height rises to 4,248 metres so it will be a great way to test our abilities and our acclimatisation before we make the final ascent of Mont Blanc. It will take several hours to climb and it will be better to start fresh, so after our long trek today we decide to bivouac in the open. And anyhow, the winds are becoming much worse and we must wait for them to die down, otherwise the climb up the Tacul would be too perilous.

The sensible idea, to me at least, seems to build our ice camp as close to the mountain as possible, so obtaining its protection from the fierce storm that is constantly buffeting us. But, as so often on the mountain, the obvious solution is the most dangerous. The mountain can shrug its shoulders whenever it chooses. The torrents of snow easily become an avalanche, and could then bury us in a matter of seconds. No one can ever foretell when an avalanche will occur, only that it may happen very suddenly. The night is always a danger time, and so we must camp in the completely exposed plateau, several hundred metres away from the mountain's slopes. The wind seems to rejoice at our decision, intensifies to gale force proportions and dances mockingly around us.

12

SIXTEEN HOURS IN THE ICE

The shovels the team are carrying now come into their own, no longer the dead weight they had seemed previously. Each is an important tool. We use them to cut into the snow floor of the ice wastes, which we then shovel into wall-blocks, building the blocks up around the holes that we are slowly creating. To keep the holes small and compact and less open to the wind, but to share any risks the night might bring, we divide into teams of two, and each take it in turn to dig out the hole until it is approximately 1 metre deep, 2 metres long and 1 metre wide. The ice is welded and heightened around the edges to provide a more solid windbreak. I flatten out the floor of the pit as much as possible, as this will be our bed through the night, but it is impossible to smooth out the smaller indentations and lumps; the hardened ice is shovel resistant, and puts up a spirited defence to my efforts. Conversation is minimal. We all know what we have to do, and it saves energy to carry out the tasks without talking. I prefer the silence, and the whiteness swirling fiercely around me removes any sense of time and all other realities. This is now.

The communal lavatory is dug some 10 metres away, and we all use it in turn, thereby hoping we will not have to use it during the night. Although I do not feel hungry I eat from my provisions, and we use the primus stoves to heat some soup. It is time to try to rest. We aim to get up at one o'clock in the morning, in the hope that the weather will permit an early climb. I remove my boots, but no more, and place the boots, the crampons and the other equipment items I expect not to need during the night inside a large plastic survival bag. I then slide my sleeping bag inside my bivouac bag, and wriggle myself inside the two. I soon come into contact with a number of the ice lumps that I haven't flattened out and that now choose to assert themselves. But at least it is very warm. I wish my sleeping companion good night and pull the flap of the bivi bag over my head. The top neatly fixes itself to the underneath, and I am totally encapsulated. I turn the miniature hand torch I carry on to my watch; it is six o'clock, at night. The light from the torch seems full of life. I am totally alone, yet feel no loneliness. There is an inner spirit in everyone.

I try to sleep. At first I think I will, and actually start to doze, but soon the sounds of the night, the un-compromising solidity of the ice and the force of the wind decide otherwise. I am very hot and try to remove one of my layers of clothing, but after struggling and becoming hotter in the process I decide against making any further effort and content myself with removing one extra pair of socks. I keep my body straight, arms at my sides and relax. I enjoy the privilege of the night, of the mountain and of nature's forces around me. Zen states 'All that is necessary is to lay down, not just the body but one's heart and the whole of oneself.' I concentrate on that thought, and feel at peace.

I have some food in a pocket, together with a litre of water in case of need, but I don't want to drink if at all possible, so as to avoid having to get up and use the lavatory we have built. I can't really face climbing out of my sleeping and bivi bags, putting on my boots, fighting my way across the ice and then back again in the wind and sub-zero temperature, after which I will have to remove my boots again and clamber back inside my sleeping bags. It is very dark as well, making it even more difficult to accomplish such tasks satisfactorily.

Suddenly I feel extremely hot. There is little air, and I am stifling. I start to fight for my breath, and try urgently to loosen the bivi top. I have covered myself in so well it proves very difficult, and I feel panicked for a few moments until I manage to open the slit at the top and can gulp in the icy-cold mountain night air. The wind is gusting with a very strong force. It rushes in and stings my eyes, whipping itself across my face. It is painful, but I need the air more, so I leave it open throughout the night and suffer with it in order to breathe more easily; I prefer the wind to the choking sensation I felt previously. I put my snow glasses on to protect my eyes, but the lenses are soon covered with a film of snowflakes, so that even with my eyes open I can see nothing. But I can still feel everything. *Ma o shimeru* means to eliminate the space in between, and that's how it feels to me. I and the night are one.

Of course it means I can't sleep, but I accept that and I am happy to stay awake, closely tuned into my surroundings. I can hear the wind, feel the urgency of the snow, the ice against my back, and I can always sense the mountains. It is as if I am totally alone, I feel no concept of another living being, even though I know another person is resting or sleeping just a few centimetres away.

Zen teaches that time does not pass in vain, it is only we who pass our time in vain. Zen also asks who is the judge, who is the expert, who is the arbitrator, in deciding what has passed in vain? Sometimes I check my watch and, despite having thought through a number of ideas, concepts or teachings, the minute hand seems to have barely moved. At other times, when it seems perhaps only one thought has occupied my mind, I find that a whole hour has passed. I can't tell whether I am the one conditioned to respond to time, or whether the idea itself is the instigator. During this period there are some moments of magic in their intensity and clarity, and I wish I could retain them or record them. Within my confined and cramped cocoon it is impossible to write, but I try to etch my thoughts deeply inside my brain. Henry Thoreau was probably the first American writer influenced by Buddhism in any form. He lived in the earlier part of the 19th century, regretfully only reaching the age of 45, but his book *Walden*, reflecting his two-year period of solitude living in the backwoods of Massachusetts, survives as a classic work. I recall his dictum, that 'You never achieve what you aim for, so aim high'. I don't know whether it can be counted as a Zen thought, but on the mountain it seems totally appropriate.

I check my watch. It is 1 a.m. The wind has not abated, perhaps it has even increased in intensity, so there seems little chance of our breaking camp and starting the Tacul climb. Further hours pass and I continue to enjoy this very special place where I am lying and the conditions I am experiencing. When I remove my snow glasses I cannot see any stars. There is still no light. Often I feel as if I am floating within the snow wastes; or rather, my mind feels as if it is floating, for my back is nearly always conscious of the hard, unforgiving ice beneath it.

There seem to be separate portions within my brain, so I am able to accommodate differing feelings within each section without losing the thoughts of the others. The wind often changes direction and intensity. Sometimes it appears almost to caress me, then a moment later will whip itself harshly across that part of my face that is left uncovered. I am in an ice hole, but I can't see the hole or the ice; it is as if I am within a great void, an emptiness beyond measure, the only man awake and seeking to be awakened in the world – certainly in my world. Zen freedom is effectively in the world, but not necessarily of the world.

I check my watch. Time continues to move strangely; sometimes only a few minutes have elapsed, other times more than an hour will have passed. I think I am searching for God's time, but I don't know what that is. Everyone has to decide alone. This place

[66]

is filled with belief. Sometimes time, space and circumstances collide. Presumably I occasionally doze, although it never seems as if I have. But eventually it is five o'clock, and I am conscious that there is light appearing. I watch it advance, slowly brightening and taking over, even though the wind never allows the day to master or calm it.

Altogether I spend some 16 hours in the ice hole. I hear the sounds and thoughts of the wildness around me, and perceive its mystical changes of intensity and wind force, its temperature extremes, its moods and emotions, and eventually its combinations of colour and vibrancy. At times I feel utterly naked; not defenceless, but always totally receptive; never threatened, but constantly aware of the mountain's powers. There is an affinity between us.

Eventually it becomes 9 a.m. Some team members appear and shout to me through the wind to break camp. Climbing the Tacul is now out of the question as it will be very hazardous, and there will be even greater chances of avalanche from the blizzard that has refused to abate during the night. So we are abandoning our climb and must make our way back to the Aiguille.

13

JULY 5 – TREKKING BACK THROUGH A BLIZZARD

Zen teaches the greatest economy of expression and action. I try to follow that dictum as I struggle in the almost overpowering winds to put on my boots and lace them tightly around my ankles. At times I have to remove my gloves to complete the fastenings, and my hands freeze quickly in the exposed and volatile conditions. Already bent over as I fold my sleeping and bivouac bags and store them within the back-pack, the wind almost forces me on to my knees. My bones ache as I complete the final preparations, adjusting the crampons that are so vital if we are to make sufficient progress back through this raging blizzard. I heave the pack on to my back and am almost bent double under its weight and the onslaught of the worsening weather. I step towards the other misted figures, also preparing themselves for the return. We look a dispirited group of individuals as we rope ourselves into the two sets of six again. There is little to say, and no one has any strength or enthusiasm to converse.

The ice holes, already half filled with snow, will vanish and be reclaimed into the white and desolate wilderness within a short time of our leaving. It is difficult to accept that I have spent the last 16 hours lying in such a shallow sanctuary. I realise how easily someone could be abandoned or abandon hope, in such bleak conditions.

The wind has created treacherous snowdrifts, and progress is very slow. We can only see a few metres ahead – we certainly can't see the Aiguille or anything else to guide us – so we rely totally on compass bearings. I continually stumble in the deepening snow. My boots are sucked downwards, and each time I pull them free takes a greater effort; it is as if I am walking in treacle or glue, a constant battle to stay upright and move forward. The storm is merciless, totally discouraging, but I don't dare pause. I have to fight constantly to maintain the will to continue. Nearly 1,200 years previously Bazo, the Zen philosopher, stated that 'In the bitterness of the wind you feel the bottom of your mind', but I never understood before the depths to which he referred. I try to relax and maintain a steady momentum, but it is almost impossible, although at times I am able to will away the tensions and strains that threaten to beat me and my spirit to the ground.

I try to economise in thought and step. Sometimes I succeed. The great cat animals know how to walk sparingly, so I try to imitate the walk of a tiger. My face is coated with snow. At times I cannot even see the person in front of me, just the end of a rope disappearing into nothingness. Sometimes the rope slackens as someone stops or stumbles or falls, and for that one or two moments it feels as if everyone has vanished, as if I am walking on my own. The tired mind plays tricks; I hear snatches of conversation, even songs, as if from the streets of a town, but it is only the wind shrieking in my ears.

The only times we stop are to check the compass. Then usually we set off in another direction, and it is obvious we have been forced away from our intended planned route. I have no means of knowing how long I will have to walk, and I don't ask. It seems preferable not to know but to accept that it will take as long as it will take. There is nothing else to do; I can't take another way, and I am not going to stop and rest, for resting is as painful as walking. I prefer to keep going and to battle with the blizzard. I will not let it win. Its howling seems demented, as if it realises my deter- mination and is frustrated at its inability to thwart my progress. Then, as if to trick us, even to beguile us, the wind suddenly stops and it seems the storm has abated. But moments later it resumes with even greater ferocity, and tries again to break our spirits. I am so tired that I do not respond to the calm or the rage, but just concentrate on taking one step forward, making each step important as part of my journey.

We are climbing all the time now, slowly, painfully, but steadily. It means we are climbing up the ice ridges towards the Aiguille and that eventually, if we keep going, we will reach it. Time has absolutely no meaning. It has been many hours since we broke camp, but it wouldn't matter if it had been only minutes, or even days. The secret, the open secret, is not to stop. The snowdrifts drag my boots to deeper depths, so that at times my legs are covered to the knees. My back throbs, but it doesn't matter, for each part of me has to deal with its own pain – my legs, my arms, my head. All that matters is my determination to go on.

As I climb I wonder if the mountain has a voice, for it seems to be speaking to me. Is it encouraging me, has it accepted me, or will it try to trap me? Perhaps the thin air is making me lightheaded. Perhaps it is a revelation. I do not try to examine my thoughts too deeply, leaving that for another time. All that matters now is to keep going forward and upward; the more I talk to myself the better, as it distracts me from the fear of failure.

Many, many hours later we reach the final narrow ice ridge that leads to the Aiguille station and to warmth and rest. *Aiguille* is French for needle, and I now know why this mountain has been so called, and what the word really means. For the ridge has been pared down by the storms and the fierce winds so that it is indeed the narrowest of edges, with steep slopes falling downwards on either side and nothing to hold on to if one should slip. There's nothing to do but proceed; there's no other way. I must force myself forward. My pace is so slow, the wind fighting to push me backwards. Sometimes I don't seem to move, and often I don't, as I have to think myself forwards along the edge of the ridge that doesn't seem to provide any support. At times the wind toys with me, and I sway sideways as I grapple to stay erect and step forward. When I look down to the valleys on either side they often seem to be compelling me to go down there, but I fight that instinct and take another step upwards. If one of us falls it's likely some others will follow, so the responsibility to oneself is also a responsibility to the rest of the team. I suddenly realise that my head is quite clear, which means that I've not experienced any altitude sickness, possibly because it's been so important to concentrate on the trek, the climb and the return.

The station appears out of the white mists. All I have to do now is to stay calm and firm in my resolve for a few minutes longer. I fight against any loss of concentration, for I know that it's often the last moments that are the most dangerous. The Zen philosopher Yoshida Kenko stated this truth in his literary notes, written in the 14th century and known as *Tsure-Zure Gusa.*

A tree rigger [tree-top lumberjack] was obviously exceptionally nervous as he neared the top of the high fir tree he was calling. No one shouted any words of caution or concern. When he had climbed down and was very near the bottom a companion said, 'Be careful now'. Later it was explained 'When someone is in danger his fear makes him exceptionally alert and capable of coping with extreme danger. Yet when he is close to safety, that makes him relax and that then becomes the moment of greatest danger.'

14

SPIRIT OF SHIN

It is the final Time. The Time to attempt the final ascents that would either lead me to the Summit or turn me around and take me down. I will know within the next few days whether I can stand the pace and live with the pressures, or succumb to the many forces opposing me. The altitudes to which I will climb will test me to my ultimate; the thinner atmosphere will place the greatest strain on my mental attitudes. My goal is 4,807 metres; nothing less will suffice.

I have endured a great deal to reach this point, this final stage, but I have also learned my physical limitations. I am not a natural climber. My lack of mountaineering technique and experience, my not having climbed before, have become all too apparent on the lower slopes, even though they were overcome. But it is not a question of fitness and climbing skills as far as I am concerned. Reliance on those alone would fail me. Only an inner spirit, a determination of will can see me through; I will be approaching and encountering several moments of truth, each of which could defeat me if my spirit is broken.

In all Japanese sports a great emphasis is laid on a person's spirit, but perhaps nowhere greater than in *sumo* wrestling. In *sumo* the three great attributes needed are technique, strength and the spirit that they call *shin*. And of all three, *shin* is the most important. *Shin*, the spirit within a person, is the driving force used to fight against the greatest odds. It has enabled some *sumo* wrestlers to overcome their lack of technique and strength, and defeat opponents who were considered superior in the other two qualities but who had a lesser *shin*. A *sumo* uses Zen techniques to attack and beat his opponent. When two *sumo* wrestlers mount the *dohyo*, the small circular ring where the contest takes place, first of all they allow their minds to grapple and to oppose, so that a contest can be won before the first blows are struck; the strength of a *sumo*'s mind, by his use of *shin*, tries to overpower that of his opponent. After this initial struggle of the minds, it is a question of technique and strength, thrust, push, push over or pull down, again and again. But, throughout, the *shin* is the greatest part of a *sumo*'s make-up; he must never give up, he should have spirit to spare. If a *sumo* is successful he eventually becomes a *yokozuna*, but he requires continuing effort, spirit and success to remain one.

As I climb some of the rock faces I use the technique of thrust, push, pull, to enable me to master rocks that seem beyond my reach and strength to conquer. My own *shin* is the special Zen ingredient I try to use to battle me to the top. Barring unforeseen accidents, barring a total inability to combat altitude sickness, I feel I have the *shin* to make it. I would like to proceed at a slower pace than is required, but I won't object; I accept the pace set, and will proceed as demanded of me.

To help my fight against possible altitude sickness, I carry extra water, over and above that carried by the others. At times I carry as much as 4 litres, and whenever there is an opportunity I replenish my water stock. The struggle up the mountain uses up the body's water constantly, and can quickly cause dehydration; it is therefore essential to replenish this loss of water as often as possible, otherwise you become light-headed and more prone to the pressures of high altitude. It means I have to carry extra weight, but the weight I am carrying anyhow seems so much beyond what I feel I can manage that the additional water seems hardly to add to the total weight, only to the unwieldy bulk, of my back-pack.

My back continually hurts if I think about it, so I choose not to think about it. My legs also ache enormously if I think abut them, so I don't. Instead my thoughts are totally concentrated on the mountain. Not the whole of Mont Blanc, but just that part where I am at any particular moment and then the next part that I need to reach. In the long treks across the glacier ridges, between the rock climbs, I remember my training technique and count to 100, then count again, and again and again. I breath rhythmically with my counting. It is using the art of *susoku*.

But it is important not to limit the mind. Some think that mind is merely thought and perception. But the

[75]

mind is also trees, plants and rocks; you can become part of them and they part of you. I need the rocks to be part of me if I am to scale them successfully. The Japanese religion of Shinto sees all things as possessing a spirit, and I feel the spirit of the mountain awakening to me.

15

JULY 6 – ASCENT TO THE TÊTE ROUSSE

We travel up part of the Aiguilles from Les Houches, but this time take the *téléphérique* cable cars over to Bellevue, 1,781 metres. From there we hike over the grassy terraces to catch the small, mountain rack-and-pinion train that will take us up higher and halfway around the mountain's lower edges, the Nid d'Aigle at 2,372 metres. We get off at the end of the line, the train retreats downwards and we start our long climb to the Tête Rousse. The way is up an extremely steep rock face, interspersed with ice patches, so that I have to react to the differing and difficult environments continually encountered.

I pick up a small stone to carry with me. If I make it to the Summit I intend to place it at the top. To me it symbolises the movements of the Earth, the way in which all parts of the mountain are equal to each other, the impermanence of it all in the story of Time. The mountain has its own time. The one is part of the whole.

The strains on my back are tremendous, and in order to move myself forward I grunt my way upwards, heaving myself on to the next rock or on to the next hand-hold. Sometimes there doesn't seem to be a hand-hold, but I know someone has climbed before me so there must be a way. Just as the right action doesn't always occur unless you are prepared to let go, so, sometimes, perhaps often, I have to jump upwards in order to grip a hand to a rock that is just out of my reach. For that exhilarating moment I feel free of the mountain, almost flying, but I am always very glad to land safely. The rocks become my friends, my support, my guide, my refuge.

I mustn't stop. There is one climber above me, setting the pace, and others behind me who seem impatient to follow. Surely they must be as tired as I am, but I don't ask and they don't volunteer.

I have to climb across the mountain first one way, then another, in a continuing zigzag pattern, following the line of the trail. At rare times I climb vertically, and occasionally I am forced to climb downwards in order to find the right direction upwards. The rocks are extremely hard and powerful, very much a part of the mountain. Then a rock or a stone loosens, and I find myself holding something that is no longer part of the mountain, the lack of support threatening to topple me away and down the mountain, with my back-pack always conspiring to assist in dragging me backwards. I have to summon every particle of strength and force my legs to oppose the downwards thrust; I clutch myself to the rock face until I am able to control my balance again. A Zen master, Tanouye Tenshin Roshi, teaches that you have to learn to push the rock where it wants to go. This thought and technique are central to all martial art procedures, and gradually I learn how to follow these instructions myself, how to know which rocks will support me and which will not. Yet I must never relax my guard. There's an old Russian proverb that states this truth: 'Doveryai no proveryai' – Trust but verify.

The final stage of the twisting route up to the Tête Rousse is an utterly exhausting climb through jutting rocks and sharp-edged ice ridges. At times we have to rope together in our two teams, and there are moments when I can feel the insistent pull of those behind as they labour over the rocks I have somehow managed to clamber over. The sun beats down on us when we are exposed to its direct rays, and we have to strip off our outer clothes, but when we are in the shade of a bluff it becomes bitterly cold. We stop several times to rest, and I gulp down some water, partly to quench my thirst but partly in an endeavour to reduce the weight of the back-pack, which now seems too heavy to manage. I also eat some chocolate, hoping it will provide me with some more energy. But there is little time at our stops for relaxation, and once the second team has caught up we start off again; if we rest too long there is a great danger our resolve may slacken and we will not be able to continue.

One of our team is having great difficulty in matching the speed set by the leader, and he asks him on a number of occasions to stop so that he can catch his breath. But when we unrope in the last sections of the climb his pace slows right down so that he drops behind, and several times we have to wait for him to reach us. The additional stops are beneficial to me but psychologically disastrous for him, because by the time he catches up with us the leader is anxious to move on and he is given little time to rest. His climb is becoming more and more desperate, it is painful to watch his struggles. I know no one can help him and that his determination must come from within. Somehow he manages to keep going and reaches the Refuge Du Tête Rousse with us, but he is exhausted mentally as well as physically. He decides he cannot continue, and will go back down the next day. I ask him not to make the decision tonight but to wait till tomorrow and see how he feels after a night's rest. I organise our sleeping bunk spaces at the Refuge; we are both pleased to crawl in alongside those already resting, and to stretch out our very weary limbs. We are so tightly packed that if one moves everyone else moves, and there is constant agitation throughout the night. Very few of us seem to fall asleep. I certainly don't.

But in the morning his feelings are the same. He has not regained his confidence, and is determined not to continue, particularly as he doesn't want to hold any of us back. I don't try to dissuade him as I know how difficult it will be on the higher sections. The first team of six is now a team of five and this seems to put an added pressure on each of us.

For a time he seems to have taken some of my own strength and determination with him. I thought he'd be one of the last to turn back; he seemed so much fitter and stronger than I am. There must have been a moment when something inside him refused to continue. I know it is there lurking inside me, and it has to be fought every step of the way, along with the opposing elements of the weather and the mountain. At times when I am spreadeagled against the rocks, wondering how to proceed, and at first seeing no possibilities, I have to think myself forward, until I can see a hold or a position that offers the way. A Zen thought states the provoking truth: 'The vertical line and the horizontal line of the body should meet and form right angles to give the perfect cross where one should be exactly in the middle.' Sometimes I achieve this, and it is a glorious feeling. Mostly I can't, but at least I know it is possible. There are many I see on the way up who show the signs of defeat on their faces, in the way they move, or the hesitation they reveal when tackling a particularly difficult piece.

In Zen it is often very important to trust without asking a question, and that sometimes means taking a calculated chance. Every action must be a positive one, made not aggressively but resolutely, always showing a total determination to succeed. It is possible to accept that success may eventually elude me, that the odds against my reaching the Summit are increasing with every metre I advance, but I must never accept the impossibility of what I am doing or I will definitely fail. It is necessary to look for inspiration, to seek encouragement, to take pleasure from everything accomplished, no matter how little. The word 'Yes' keeps ringing in my ears, even though the word 'No' is never far behind. 'Yes I will climb higher.' 'Yes a little more.' 'Yes a bit further.' 'Yes I'll try again and again.'

Without ever expecting ultimate defeat, I do not think it necessary to plan and expect to reach the Summit. I treat each few metres as a smaller summit, so that each small ascent is a victory to be recorded. Each step has its own meaning and is important in its own right. There is a Zen saying that I hold close to me: 'Thousands of repetitions, and out of one's true self perfection emerges.' It is the way forward. It is *sando*, the Way of the mountain.

With one team member less, I have become more aware how much each of us is vulnerable. Any one of us may be the next to stop, to turn back from the goal that never seems to get very much nearer. The more I climb, the more strenuous is the effort and resolve needed. There seems to be a strange link between the height ascended and the mental and physical pressures endured. The mountain always maintains the upper hand.

16

JULY 7 – THE MOUNTAIN SPEAKS

Early that morning we leave the Tête Rousse, 3,167 metres, cross the Grand Couloir and climb steadily upwards. It's steeper, much rockier and possibly more dangerous than the previous rock climbs. I know I must try not to fight the mountain, but work with it, try to read it, try to live it. The rocks are very large and bulky so that they are more difficult to climb over. At times I have to rest myself, arms curved around a jutting rock, so I feel almost suspended in space, leaning out from the mountain, with no real support underneath me, relying on the strength of my arms and the grip of my ice axe. Small stones tumble loose as I climb, and I am as concerned about hitting someone below me as I am about being hit myself. I am constantly reminded how vulnerable we all are, even though we are often roped together; in addition to the climbing rope, it is as if there is also an unseen silken rope that binds the team with its shared desire to complete the climb successfully. Perhaps this is why I have been feeling so depressed during the last few hours; the member of our team who had to give up and descend was one of us, a part of us; his loss was our loss, his failure was our failure. The mountain has taught me that lesson; whatever else happens, it is a moment of insight for which I am grateful. I don't express it to the others; I hope they are feeling it as well, but if they are not then there would be no point in stating it myself. The silence within and around us is total; it expresses everything that is needed. No spoken language is required. Speech is totally irrelevant; only feelings matter up here.

We finally leave the rocks and reach the upper glaciers. I know that we have now moved up on to the neck of the mountain and are straining to reach its face and to touch its head. Here we have to put on our crampons and keep them on all the time, otherwise the mountain could easily shake us off, and should that happen there is little to stop us sliding and crashing, perhaps falling, all the way down. The edges of the crampons look like prehistoric animals' teeth, and fit in well with the barren and hostile region we are in; it is as if we are transported back in time to an age before civilisation, when only Man, Woman and Nature existed. We are without any form of artificial communication – I have seen no one with a radio or even with a music headset.

It is as if everyone has to accept the terms of the mountain. 'Come to me if you must, climb me if you dare, but leave the other world far behind.' I can feel everything, or choose not to feel anything. My mind is totally detached. Perhaps it's the lack of oxygen. My feelings are not of today or tomorrow, but of the millions of yesterdays that make up the mountain. The mountain continues to speak to me.

Respect me and you may live. Ignore me and face peril. Your axes, your boots, your poles, do not hurt me. I can feel no pain. But insult me and I will shake myself and let loose my own words. Beneath the ice, beneath the rocks, beats my heart. But my head is not at the head; the mountain should not be judged as you judge other things. You may start at any point but that is not the bottom. You may reach to any point but that is not the top. Stand back and think again, and you see that you cannot see. There is no beginning, there is no end. Just remember to tread warily. I do not invite you. I will not object to your presence, but do not stay too long in case I weary of you. Those that stay too long may not leave, yet will not remain.

It is very much colder. I put on some extra clothing, but the coldness still penetrates. In a way it helps. I want to stop, but only by continuing can I keep warm, or at least keep a little warmer. I bruise both elbows several times in grappling to keep myself from slipping.

I am now in some kind of half-animated state. Each step is one of strain and pain, my leg and arm muscles complaining, my back aching and protesting. But their protests are muffled, as if coming from someone else a long way off, as if realising they will not be heeded. I try to maintain a rhythm to help me keep up the pace, but find it very difficult, for the terrain constantly changes and reacts differently to me as I proceed upwards. I know it is essential, though, so I persevere. I accomplish things that I didn't realise would ever be possible. I stretch my legs to points beyond their usual limitations. I hold my body weight and my back-pack with one arm whilst the other searches for another hold. Each movement I make must lead to the next. I try to climb within a momentum of movements that are linked, so that there is no break in my continuity. This is very much the Zen way of pursuing an activity. *Zanshin* is where the force, the *shin*, remains with you, alert at all times, and is carried through from one movement or activity to the next, and then on again to the next. The energy must be kept flowing without interruption, so a rhythm of *shin* is created. With true *zanshin* an accident will not rob you of your *shin*; you will overcome it and move immediately on to the next correct step. I am resolved to keep going no matter what I must endure.

Some hours later, possibly – I've completely lost count of real time — we reach the Refuge du Goûter, the very last place to stop before the final assault on the top. I refuse to acknowledge the pains that try to demand my attention. It's time to look down on the clouds and then to look up.

17

JULY 8 – ANXIOUS TIMES AT THE REFUGE du GOÛTER

The Refuge du Goûter is our final stop, high above the cloud line, where the clouds often cover everything in sight, underlining the sense of isolation. It is truly a refuge in so many senses of the word. Arriving there is like reaching the furthest outpost in the Arctic wastes, prior to heading finally to the North Pole itself. It's a shack, no more than a wooden hut, set up as the final stopover before the final ascent. I feel its presence, its sanctity. I know that it carries within it the memories, the successes and the failures, of the many climbers who have used it in previous years. But it does not judge. It is a sanctuary, a resting place, a place to practise one's art, a place for Zen. The house where one goes to study Zen is a *dojo*, so this refuge will be my *dojo* for as long as I use it. Its sparseness and lack of facilities will help me to practise Zazen, for I must concentrate with all my mental strength if the last climb, the final trek to the Summit, is to be achieved.

Inside, the refuge is crammed with climbers from every nation in the world, yet all sharing a common ideology – the desire to climb to the Summit of Mont Blanc. That desire pervades everything. Conversation is limited. Zen guards against over-emphasising the value of words: direct experience and action are all important. Everyone here is concentrating on his or her motivation, on trying to remain self-contained. There are a few sleeping rooms, each with two levels of long, communal bunk beds. But they were all booked long ago, and latecomers like myself have little chance of hiring a bunk-bed space. I can sleep on the floor, though, after lights are turned out at about 9 p.m., an offer I gladly accept. The alternative is to sleep outside and dig another ice hole. Some prefer the latter, knowing that an overcrowded hut can mean a poor night's rest and bad start in the morning, but I know that a night in an ice hole would do little to ease my back pain, and I need every extra chance if I'm to make it to the Summit. There are no washing facilities at the refuge either, but I am able to purchase some bottled water to drink, bringing my stock back up to 4 litres. I feel I am going to need it. Others are lightening their loads, but I'd rather have more water than I might need in order to give me a greater chance of fighting against the altitude sickness. Several climbers are suffering badly, and I can see that they won't make it to the top. Just the sight of their present difficulties persuades me to drink nearly half a litre of water immediately, and I purchase more to top up again.

The lavatories are extremely primitive, but I make use of them, hoping I can pass the night without having to use them again. They are two small adjoining wooden huts, some distance away, perhaps 60 metres, on the side of the mountain, looking as if a strong wind would easily topple them into the valleys so very far below. One of the huts has a nail on one wall, making it far superior to the other; it means I can hang my jacket and ski poles on the nail in comparative safety, with little risk of them falling through the gaping floor hole where there would be no chance of retrieving them. The way back up from the huts to the refuge is icy, treacherous and extremely slippery, and several times I have to force a ski pole heavily into the ice to prevent myself from tumbling.

The weather reports come through regularly, every few hours throughout the day. At the Summit conditions are very bad and unpredictable. Anyone climbing would be risking their own lives, those of their team mates and possibly the lives of those who may be needed to search for anyone subsequently missing. It would be foolhardy to chance climbing today, and possibly even tomorrow. Yet it is also possible that the weather may not change for days. This is most depressing news, as I am booked to fly out from Geneva airport in three days time. I decide that after having come so far and made such efforts, I will not leave the mountain until I am given a chance to make it to the top. Some of the other climbers look and sound totally desperate, and I guess they only have tomorrow to climb. I expect that some will attempt it no matter how dangerous that may be; the lure of the mountain is too strong and the trauma of having to descend without the opportunity to try for the top is almost too much to bear. The adverse and changing weather conditions are one of the main reasons why Mont Blanc claims so many lives each year, and why there are so many accidents; the mountain thwarts the climber, the climber tries to fight back, but the mountain usually wins.

I can feel the call of the mountain myself; I have to fight down my own impatience, to think through calmly the prospects for a successful final assault. I will not be panicked into going too soon; I will wait out the time, no matter what. We all check the weather reports as they come in, and agree to make a decision on whether to climb only when we know that the conditions are likely to remain stable.

I settle down to wait. At least I have my Zen notebook with me. I read it through, adding some more notes. They are a calming influence. I realise that whilst I wait I could practise my climbing techniques on the glaciers and ice ridges around the refuge. Of course I know I should be doing this, but somehow I can't bring myself to leave the hut. I feel I am in limbo, a metaphysical existence that has no constancy of effect. It is like waiting for a momentous event, an earthquake, being prepared for its eventuality, but not knowing when it is finally to take place. I feel neither here nor there. I find it difficult either to explain or to deal with my changing moods or emotions; I wait for time to move on at its own pace and for the decision to be made for me by a process of natural evolution. I am not the master of my own destiny: the mountain is. I am aware more than ever how insignificant I am at this moment. I feel that the mountain has a majestic power, an overwhelming force, that overrides every-thing and everyone. Many hours pass. I try to fight away the impatience that threatens to break through.

I find that time runs both fast and slow; it is not constant, but reacts and relates to activity and thought, existing around and within each of them. I feel frozen within space, waiting for some outside force to strip an outer shell and release me. I fight my way back to reality and shake off the negative thoughts that have tried to swamp me. I look at the pale, strained, unshaven and unwashed faces around me, and feel that they are pulling me downwards to an unknown depth. I must get out from the refuge for a short while.

I put on my jacket, pull on my boots and step outside. Standing on the edge of the ice rim, looking down into the valley, I can see far below a group of helmeted climbers, laboriously making their way up to us, their helmets and brightly coloured anoraks and packs vividly standing out from the grey and sombre tones of the rocks and stones over which they are toiling. They are all roped together, very slowly snaking up the mountainside. It's illuminating to see how slowly they seem to move upwards; I can sense the tremendous effort they have to make with every step, and am made aware how much effort it must have cost me to cover the same distance. There is no sound on the mountain. I feel as if I'm watching a silent movie being acted out in slow motion; when the climbers pause, an unseen film director – perhaps it is me – shouts 'Cut', and when they recommence he shouts 'Action'. They have heard no words, but they have understood. The climbers dislodge some rocks, and rock dust momentarily hides them; it brings home to me the value of wearing a helmet and the folly of my not using one.

I walk around the refuge to stare up at the mountain, but its pyramid shape makes it impossible for me to see more than a few hundred metres up the slope. This is one of the ways the mountain continually draws you upwards. As you're climbing you never see the Summit until you are almost at the top itself. You are never certain how far there is to go, for how much longer you may still have to climb. If you give up you might find that you had been just a short distance from your goal. Some climbers and ice explorers have missed their destination in this way by just a few metres. It is like missing a race record by a few seconds; you will always think you could have made it if only you'd known it was that close. But that is part of the challenge of the mountain; the uncertainty of it, not knowing how far there is yet to go, pushing on for a few metres more, a few steps more. Pushing oneself beyond one's limitations. That is such a part of Zen. Never accepting limitations. It is not a rebellion against order or clarity or society, but rather an internal conflict within oneself, always trying to achieve one's utmost and then extending even beyond that.

Later during that very long day the news is at last received that everyone has been waiting for. The weather is stabilising at the top and we can reasonably start the climb the next morning. There is a joyous and feverish reaction from those climbers waiting in the refuge.

Everyone is excited, then a calmer reaction sets in. Our fears can't be expressed, but we all know that at long last we are all to undergo the final test. It is for this reason that I have come to the mountain. I feel sorry for the few who have already had to accept defeat, for whatever reason – altitude sickness, lack of stamina, lack of preparedness; they will now descend or wait at the refuge for the outcome of their companions' efforts. But it is not a time for negative thoughts, and I try to maintain my inner excitement, and to keep myself keyed up for tomorrow's challenge. For the first time I realise how immensely tired I am, how much the ascent thus far has taken out of me.

I decide to eat more of my provisions to try and replenish my energy levels. Eating a meal can be a practice of Zen, and I try to make it so. Tozan said 'When I am hungry I eat, when I am thirsty I drink, when I am tired I sleep.' When you are hungry there is real pleasure in the plainest of foods, and I savour every mouthful. I know the energy from the food will be part of my life-line on the climb tomorrow; it is as vital an ingredient as my effort and determination. Tea drinking can also be part of the Zen preparations, an art form in its own right; it is a symbolic way of waiting for the right time to come around, the time for decision or of challenge.

I also decide to go to sleep immediately, or at least to rest my body and my mind. Both have been operating at such a level of high activity that I need to calm them. Other climbers have the same idea. Soon most of us are stretched out, side by side, breathing steadily and deeply. I concentrate, using the greatest effort, in order to reach a state of intensity that will allow tomorrow's ascent to be achieved. Whether from this or from physical exhaustion, I fall into a deep sleep.

I wake up with a start. It is pitch black. I can see nothing. As I start to fall asleep again I hear the mountain calling. Is it insanity? I know that at times like these anything can occur. Ingenuity, courage, perseverance, sacrifice are just some of the inner traits that reveal themselves at times of greatest determination. I feel very determined, willing to face tomorrow as it presents itself. I recall some words of Zen Master Yuanwu: 'The Way is arrived at by enlightenment. The first priority is to establish resolve.' I know I must seek a balance between the tranquility of the mind and its resolution not to be deterred from the Way. Yuanwu also stated that 'As soon as you try to chase and grab Zen, you've already stumbled past it.' I must try not to stumble tomorrow.

I feel the actual moment I am asleep.

18

JULY 9 – FINAL ASCENT

For the very first time during my time on the mountain I don't wake up early. In fact I oversleep, and it is only the sounds of the other climbers clambering noisily from the top bunks and trying to dress that awakens me. I feel hot and feverish, and am in a half-dazed state as I try to shake myself fully awake. I hurriedly pull on all the clothing I had taken off the night before, and jump down from the bunk. It is just after 2 a.m. There seem to be more people struggling to dress in the dimly lit refuge than I saw the previous night. Perhaps this is because practically everyone is now inside rather than some waiting outside. Everyone is standing up, busily pulling on clothes, checking their equipment, completing the final packing, jettisoning anything that isn't thought essential. It is a melée of bodies, with everyone frantically trying to get into a final state of readiness. I remember the advice that someone had given me, about it being preferable to bivouac outside in the ice, able to prepare in comparative quiet, rather than being involved in the pushing and shoving inside the refuge, but it's too late to change the situation now. At all costs I must stay relaxed and calm.

A small breakfast is available, and I drink tea and eat some slices of bread. I don't feel like eating, but I think it is necessary; I treat it as part of my final Zen preparations. The tea is given in a bowl, and I clasp both hands around it and raise it to my lips, letting the tea run down my throat. I haven't put in any sugar, but it tastes sweet. I place the bowl down carefully on the rough, well-worn table, and bow my head in a few moments of meditation. The sounds of the room fade and I can hear nothing but a strange whistling noise. It is something or someone calling to me, but I have no idea what or who. It is time to go and find out.

At 3 a.m. I am outside, roped to four others and ready for the final stage. The air is black and silent, very little light available, the snow and ice appearing grey and forbidding. I turn on my head-torch, but the light it gives out is small and penetrates only weakly ahead. Some climbers have already set off and I can see their minute torchlights zigzagging across the mountain slopes. I can't see the climbers themselves. The air is bitterly cold and I shiver, in spite of the number of layers of clothing I am wearing. I feel myself apart from everything I've known before. It's as if everything I possess is on my back; the food, the water, the pack are all I know for certain. I must think only of the mountain. My relationship cannot be with any of the other climbers; I can only climb alone, my relationship solely with the mountain.

We set off slowly, trying to set up a rhythm, using our ski poles to balance. My legs feel heavier than I have ever known before; it is as if they are resisting, trying to turn me back and downwards. The air seems to thin very quickly as I proceed. I am very conscious of the increasing weight of my back-pack, almost with every step I make. We are like ghosts treading on the mountain, and I sense around me the ghosts of those who have climbed before. It is truly another world; more than ever before, I am leaving everything of my material world far behind me and am stepping into unknown territory.

The first hour's climbing is very arduous. *Sesshin* means the collecting of the spirit, and it is only by continually making such a supreme effort of marathon intensity that I am able to continue. But I will fight on. I remember a Zen instruction: 'Die hard, never give up.' I need to concentrate my forces, to fight against any weakening of resolve. Zen is supreme. My *shin* speaks to me.

I recall my original running and training schedule, carried out such a long time ago in an almost forgotten place. Using my number mantra I count out my steps up to 100, then count again and yet again. Gradually I relax, loosen myself mentally, easing the pressures. My efforts become less laboured and I reach a rhythm; it courses through my legs, and they bear my weight and the weight of the back-pack more comfortably. Zen Master Foyan's words illuminate the way: 'Zen practice requires detachment from thought, this is the best way to save energy.' There is a faint glow of light ahead.

The dawn arrives, and with it the wild beauty that exists beneath the blackness of night. I feel the mountain respond to me. Perhaps it has finally decided to welcome me to it, to encourage me forward; it wants me to learn its secrets. It is necessary in Zen to recognise instinctively the moment of action, and I try to match myself to the mountain in feeling and instinct. I feel a special joy; I do not try to analyse it but prefer just to accept it graciously and gratefully.

We have been climbing now for over two hours. With the daylight I become aware that I am in a broken line of climbers. A few teams I can see above me, but they vanish quickly from sight as they reach another ridge that angles them further towards the Summit. Many more teams stretch out far below. We climb past some climbers who have decided to take it more slowly and need to rest. I would like to stop as well, but equally I want to go on. I am pleased each time I fight back the urge to ask for a stop. The greeting to give to others in Japanese is *Konnichi wa*, but I haven't the available breath to spare, so I think the word as I pass more mountaineers coming down or back or resting. I also think 'Good luck' and 'Bon chance' to them, hoping that in some way they will pick up my thoughts of encouragement. I cannot know what language they will understand; on the mountain, under knitted balaclavas, gaudy helmets, sometimes impenetrable goggles, tightly wrapped coats, it's almost impossible to guess other climbers' nationalities. On the mountain there is only one language, and we all try to speak it as best we can.

Those below me help to spur me on, perhaps

through my knowledge that they have yet to climb to the place that I have now reached. It is always hard work, very hard, but I feel I can and will make it. There is no other way to continue. There are so many times, so many places, where I could give up if I weaken, even a little, in my resolve. Yes, I must not give up. Yes, I will not give up. I enjoy the thoughts of the seeming contradiction in the words; I tussle with it for a little while, and find I have moved on again a further 100 metres. I feel the cold pricking at my forehead, like a thousand tiny bolts of electricity, constantly charging and retreating. I am utterly exposed to the elements of the mountain; this is truly its kingdom.

Every so often I glance around me. The sun is a pale liquid-gold disc, looking as if at any moment an unseen hand might tilt it and cause it to melt the ice below. The beauty is so superb, so inspiring, that my spirits lift me. I want desperately to reach the top; there I'll have time fully to drink in the sheer ecstasy the mountain offers. It's as if I have become truly part of the mountain, a working willing partner, harnessed to its energies, subject to its temperament, always conscious of its majesty. I gain a growing awareness of the mountain with every pace I take, and although the difficulties increase and the strain intensifies, I am completely content to be there. I feel totally prepared to battle on to the end.

We are climbing more slowly, but steadfastly, every person an island as well as part of the team. The snow is surprisingly thick and deep on the upper slopes; my feet often sink in, and it seems to require a greater effort each time to pull them out. I have tied my ski poles to my pack, and only use my ice axe to stabilise myself or to hack occasionally at the ice to obtain a hand-hold when I'm in danger of slipping. The ice ridges are so narrow and steep I am often in danger of toppling over, and I have to fight to balance and prevent myself sliding downwards. Sometimes the ice actually gives way; I start to fall, and have to struggle with every aching sinew to hold myself to the mountain and not freefall all the way down.

I cannot see any other climbers now. I am not conscious of my team climbers, or even of the ropes binding us. There is nothing except the mountain and my closeness to it. It's important in Zen to aim beyond one's goal. When one climbs to the top one should just keep on going. Never aim for the top, aim beyond it. The only way I can aim beyond the Summit is to fly. If only I could. These thoughts continue all the way. Sometimes my feelings soar far ahead of me, and I imagine what it will feel like when I reach the Summit. At other times I am conscious of an immense pressure holding me back, trying to push me downwards, against which I have to push forward with all my strength. But it doesn't really matter. I won't let anything defeat me. I know I will make it, I just don't know when and how. I would like more time to think about the why, but not now, that's for afterwards. There'll be plenty of time then for my reflections.

Wait! The Summit is in sight. I have 50 metres to go! My feet fly forward. I am soaring.

19

FEELING THE SUMMIT

I am on the highest ice ridge of Mont Blanc, the Summit of the mountain. I wait. But I don't have to wait very long.

The mountain speaks to me, or is it the wise man? 'Welcome. It's been such a long time. Is it worth it? Really worth it?' I think deeply, quickly, and the affirmative words of acceptance seem to float above the mountain. 'Yes, a hundred times. Yes, a thousand times. Yes, for ever.' My words – the mountain's words – take off in free flight and echo all the way down to the far-away valleys, at first falling and rising slowly, then more swiftly, laughing and crying, a mix of wonderful thoughts, feelings and emotions, finally revealing a calm that becomes the most important emotion of all. This calmness is temporary and could never be described as peace; it is a feeling, a mood, far beyond that of peace. In fact there is and could be no peace. The mountain is always fierce, to the extreme; that is part of its power and strength. Beneath its surface the fierceness lies slumbering; it is like a wild animal, sleek, soft, beautiful, but always you are conscious of the terrible power that can be unleashed should the mountain choose.

This is the moment I have longed for. I can ask all the questions I have stored within me. Will the mountain provide the answers, even just one of them? Will a question be answered with a question? Should I question an answer, perhaps with another question? Suddenly I realise that I have no questions to ask. Can I again hear the sound of one hand clapping? I marvel again at the wonderful koan that has always seemed so intricate and complex, yet now seems so full of simplicity. In Zen, wisdom is *prajna*. If I no longer need to ask a question, I feel that my climb has brought me *prajna*. Is that a question in itself?

I take from my pocket the small stone I have carried with me from the lower part of the mountain. I place it at the Summit, knowing that shortly it will disappear below the ice, either remaining hidden there, or perhaps finding its way back to its original place. It will never disappear from the mountain; it will disappear from my sight and the sight of others, but at some time it will reappear. To own a piece of the mountain is impossible. If you take away a stone or rock it ceases to be part of the mountain. Only on the mountain is it one with the mountain. No one should own a mountain — no pocket is large enough. The mountain will always outlast.

To experience Nowness is real Zen. That is the true benefit of the climb. Through the climb I have gained enlightenment. It is true *satori* Zen. Even if it is only temporary, I feel uplifted, my heart swelling to fill my body, my *shin* lifting me higher. I am experiencing the high of sheer spiritual joy. It is a feeling of ecstasy that spreads rapidly throughout my body; I feel myself lift skywards and start to float over the Summit itself. I can no longer feel anything, no part of myself, neither the harsh clothes nor the heavy equipment that has helped me to this special place. All is in my mind, and it is free of all restraints. This is why some men and women climb, why they are not prepared to give up, why they are prepared to suffer so many hardships along the way. I want to shout it out, but my voice is stilled. The moment becomes bigger than anything else, and I have to let it express itself as it will. I feel my feet touching the ground again; I lock myself to the mountain, and drink deeply.

There is a scattered line of small white clouds circling a section of the mountain, far below me, and I watch as they dance and move, forming into long, curving lines before separating once again into soft white balls of fun and mischief. The initial whiteness of the ice stretches in all directions. White is the colour of Japanese Shinto; it is the colour of purity, standing for everything that is true and fresh and new. I am here for the first time; everything around me is for the first time. It is so alive; it vibrates and glows.

I hadn't realised just how many other colours there are in snow. Blues of all the shades; golds and silvers that vie with one another; purple, pink, even green and yellow. No camera can do it justice. Only a great artist, someone like Claude Monet perhaps, could capture the interplay of light and movement that is the silent music of the inner mind. Monet painted a series of canvases in Norway, in 1895; all the pictures portrayed the same scene of Mount Kolsaas, but each encapsulated a separate and total expression of beauty and feeling, developed in the intense way that Monet painted all his subjects, revealing the mountain's specialness at one unique moment in its existence. But what dreams would Monet have realised if he could have painted Mont Blanc through some of its changes? Here I am, almost 100 years later, marvelling at the magical qualities that a mountain offers those who dare to see.

There are many sights to observe here. I walk along the Summit's narrow uppermost ridge, first to the end, then back again to the beginning – or is it the end? Then I change my position several times, all the while trying to understand what I am doing here and why it has occurred. Suddenly I can feel the intense bitterness of the wind, and realise that during all these wonderful moments of insight and awareness I am subject to freezing blasts of icy air. The wind will not permit me to remain here long. I can climb to the top; I can enjoy, and even be part of, the mountain; but my time here is limited. I have to understand and accept my impermanence here.

Life can be like a dream. Time passes so very swiftly, unless you can slow it down by making a moment very special and lasting, making it intense, intensive, full of many meanings. I fight to stretch these moments out. I succeed only for a short time, then the mountain fights back; it has decided we've been there long enough. Time is running again. We must leave. I look at my watch. It is 8.30 a.m. The date is July 9. The year is 1990. I see those figures written in the snow, then slowly they sink downwards and are gone. I remove my gloves, and with a bare finger trace the word *sando* in the snow, my word for the Way of the mountain. The word remains frozen in time and space. Only I understand what the indentations mean. It is heady stuff. I feel close to tears, but I won't let that happen. This is not the place.

The mountain is forcing me to go down, now, before it claims me totally. And if that happens I will not be allowed to return. I have to decide right now. The choice is mine. It is a moment of intense sadness, a moment that lasts and lasts. Reluctantly I whisper my goodbyes. I feel the mountain's answer, then another I can barely hear, then another, too many now even to comprehend. I can carry them away with me, though, and perhaps later I will understand. I remember the *I Ching* saying: 'After the dragon has soared to the Summit he can only know the regret of descent.'

20

DESCENDING THE GLACIERS

We agree to climb down through the glaciers, this time avoiding the rock faces and the volatile stones. Initially it looks the easier way. We are told our triumph will carry us straight through. If we are prepared to attempt it we can make our descent to Chamonix in just one day, giving us a chance to catch up on some of our lost time. We all agree to accept the challenge, another challenge. We are so exhilarated we will descend at speed and ignore our exhaustion.

I feel we are entering dangerous zones. I want to give a warning, but I know that is not the way. If I want to retain some of what I have learned, some of what I have gained, I feel I have to leave everyone their own freedom to choose and decide. Freedom is the essence of Zen. Zen liberation is achieved by special knowledge and perception that penetrates to the root of experience. Zen master Yuanwu warned, 'How could anyone show off and claim to have attained Zen.'

At first our pace is fast and steady. We have nothing to fear from the altitude now, and we gather strength and stability as we descend quickly to the lower slopes. The ice is hard and firm; we step purposefully and forcefully on it and it seems respectful, as if acknowledging our victory. What is there to fear now?

The snow stretches out before me, pristine, smooth, inviting. It seems to be smiling, almost laughing. Its invitation fools me completely. I take one step on to the ice. At first it holds, but then it breaks through and there is nothing below. My foot disappears, then my leg, my thigh following, before I am able to throw myself sideways and stab my ice axe to one side to prevent any further fall. My leg has twisted and my knee is full of pain. With the greatest efforts I pull myself clear and take stock of myself. The fall has aggravated the torn ligaments, which have never fully healed. I am full of fatigue. The mountain has staked its claim. I know now the way down will be as great a test of my resolve as the ascent, perhaps more so. I have achieved the Summit; no real motivation remains.

I also realise how really exhausted I am. My limbs will no longer easily obey the commands from my brain. I have always known that climbers die on Mont Blanc, but it suddenly strikes me that most die on the climb down, when it's easier to make a fatal mistake. When your judgment is tired and faulty there is more likelihood of an accident occurring due to slower responses; this is the Zen warning that I have been given before but have not taken fully to heart. When asked what is the living meaning of Zen, the Zen

[*107*]

master Xuedou had replied 'The mountains are high, the oceans are wide.' He could have been with me here, wondering if I have the resolve to continue.

I will not give in. I fight to re-assert my *shin* and gradually it comes through. Time has no consequence. There is nothing to beat except myself. I take a slow step forward, and again feel my foot starting to sink down, twisting my leg as I quickly pull it free. The pain in my knee intensifies. Very well, I will use the pain to strengthen me. It sears my brain; it refuses to allow me to relax. I have to stay alert at all times. I can't put too much weight on the weak leg, so I turn sideways and start to sidestep downwards. It isn't an elegant way to descend, but elegance hasn't been part of my climb from the outset. When practising meditation, Zen monks are sometimes supervised by a *jiki jitsu* who holds a stick known as *keisaku*. Just as the *jiki jitsu* will strike someone to relieve cramp, to help concentration or to transfer pain elsewhere in the body, so I use a ski pole as *keisaku* to transfer the thought of pain away from my knee. It helps, but does not work totally.

Surprisingly, even though I am experiencing so much difficulty in the descent, more so than with the ascent, I am still able to gain so much from my surreal surroundings. The snow and ice are carved with exquisite artistry into strange shapes, weird figures; the beauty is astounding. The whiteness of the ice is dazzling, and the sun is so hot I have to strip off most of my upper clothes and tie them to my pack. My back doesn't seem to feel the weight it is carrying; in fact all I can feel are my legs from my knees to the feet, and my head from the eyes upwards to my brain. Everything else no longer seems to exist. There is time for reflection. At times it is as if someone else is doing all the hard work and I am coming along as an approving companion. In some strange way I am enjoying myself. Perhaps I am still suffering from the effects of the high altitudes; perhaps we are descending too fast. It doesn't matter. I am alive and there is work to do. I must keep on travelling the path that I am creating.

I keep my movements to a rhythm, sometimes counting, always looking, sometimes exclaiming out loud. We are all still roped together; I am in the first team of five, followed some 20 minutes later by the second team of six. There are still constant dangers from hidden crevasses, and every so often someone falls and jerks the others to a painful and disturbing halt. I come across many crevasses myself, that seem to lie in wait for me, hungry mouths wide open in the ice. Some are possibly 60 metres deep, although usually less than 1 metre wide. The only way across is to jump. The width does not seem too great, but carrying a heavy back-pack, my legs and mind tiring rapidly, with the knowledge that a crevasse might extend right under the ice in any direction, means that each jump has to be an act of faith. It is now difficult to bend either of my knees, so I jump high, then, as I reach the other side, I lean forward like a skier taking off in a downhill race and dig my ice poles in the ice to propel me further forward. The moments in the air are strange and revealing, each one a test of nerve. I feel very much apart. Sometimes my ice poles do not grip, I feel myself starting to fall and have to struggle to stay upright, for falling and then getting up is very painful. Usually I manage it, but there is always the expectation I won't.

It is a long way climbing down through the glaciers, and I don't stop unless forced to. I am hobbling now, although the pain is manageable. I walk with a stubbornness that is not matched by my strength or technique. I am using the spirit of *shin* to get me through. I wonder how many times one lives and how many times one dies on the mountain. I am content to keep moving on, taking each defeat as another challenge to be overcome. Life is infinitely more complex and beautiful than it is ever possible to comprehend.

We reach the bottom of the glaciers, and it appears the worst is now over. The five of us unrope and we stop and wait for the other six to catch us up. We can then descend the remaining rock slopes together, a comparatively short distance, and be collected in the jeep and taken back to the chalet. However I very much want to spend my remaining time on the mountain alone, without the contact of others, so it's agreed that I needn't wait and can descend by myself, making my own way down as I choose.

I set off along a curving rocky pathway that leads sideways around the mountain, winding its way in a twisting convoluted fashion, often seeming to turn back on itself. It sometimes falls away steeply, then perhaps rises to an almost perpendicular wall that has to be scaled. Often it passes across torrents of icy cold water that rush headlong downwards, fed by the melting snow line. The terrain becomes slushy and unstable, and my boots are soon soaking wet. The path frequently peters out amid rocks and rough, hardened ground, so I have to guess the way, then try to find the path again, some hundreds of metres further on. Once I am confronted by a sheer rock wall and I have to climb it without knowing if this is the right way to proceed or whether I've mistaken the route. An occasional bird, a chough I think, swoops overhead; otherwise there is no sign of life. But the mountain is alive; it is life, and so it will continue. But so will I. My determination to go on is re-affirmed.

Eventually, far off in the distance, I see the overhead wires of the *téléphérique* cable-car system, and this spurs me on. I know I must be heading somehow in the right direction. I have now lost the path totally, but I think there must be a way down if I head for the cable wires, so I start to climb in that direction. But the way becomes even more rugged and difficult. I am crossing over ice gullies, stony terrain, and make several perilous scrambles along the edge of the mountain. I am heading into a rock gully and have to climb over several large rocks, my knees taking a tremendous strain, my back aching from the weight of the pack. I have hung the crampons and waist harness over the ice axe and strapped them to my pack, and they jangle as I proceed. I use the ski poles as levers to help me. Now I can't find the continuation of the path, and can't see any other climbers; the only way seems to be to follow the overhead cable wires down the valley, for I assume that they will eventually lead me to a cable-car station.

The way becomes rockier and rockier. I have to clamber over huge boulders that have fallen down the valley many years previously. It becomes a continual climb over rocks, one after another. I reach a high ridge and climb laboriously up it. At the top I look down to check my position and progress, and find I am in the middle of a massive rock valley stretching away in all directions. I have taken completely the wrong route. I should have climbed upwards and taken what had seemed at the time the long way around the mountain edge until I reached a mountain path of sorts. But it is now too far to go back, and much too difficult and exhausting to scale those huge boulders again.

I want to give up and lie down amongst the rocks and sleep, although I know I mustn't; it can be fatal to be trapped in the rocks in the dark, especially as the temperature drops so dramatically at night. So I set off again across the stone valley, aiming to reach the far side of the mountain wall so that I can try to scale it and reach the pathway above. It is past five in the afternoon. I see a cable-car slowly making its way down, and hope there will be one later. I continue to climb, now in great pain, the rocks shifting ponderously under my feet. I fall several times. If I injure myself and am unable to continue it is unlikely anyone will find me. A rock slides under my weight, my boot slips and the rock's weight crushes it painfully. Laboriously I extricate my leg, try to detach my mind, ignore the pain, and slowly climb on. I need to use *shin* more than ever. I refuse to rest. I continue to climb over some massive boulders, and toil up several sky high ridges until I reach the wall of the mountain. It looks almost impossible to climb, certainly in my condition and still carrying the weight of my back-pack. I think about leaving my pack behind, but don't want to let it go. It has been with me throughout my ascent of Mont Blanc; I have kept it with me always, and I don't want to abandon it now; it is part of me, part of the climb, and it deserves to be carried to the end, whatever the end will be.

The mountainside is now covered in loose earth, and it slides away as I clamber up it. Many times the stones I grip and lean on for support come away in my hands, and I slither down a few feet until I manage to hold on to the mountain face. I am soon covered in dust and dirt. I near the top. There is the pathway, but I see it is littered with rocks and has been abandoned, presumably as being too dangerous because of the rock falls. However there is little choice but to use it, so I pick my way gingerly over the rocks and stones, following the winding path upwards until finally reaching the top ridge that at last leads me to the cable-car station.

I look as if I've come from another world; indeed, I have come from another world. My face is gaunt and blackened. There is blood on my forehead and on my left hand from my falls among the rocks. There are tears in my over-trousers, and my boots are indented and scratched a thousand times. I feel and sound delirious as I learn that there is still one last cable-car that will shortly descend to Chamonix station. I squat against a wall, oblivious of those around me, and gulp down the last of my precious water; it tastes like the most delicious elixir.

I have made it to the top and back. My spirit soars for one final look at where I've been. It is my last farewell to the mountain, and I mouth silently my thanks and my admiration. I cannot express easily what I feel, but I know that the mountain understands. In a strange way the mountain has been my *sensei*, my teacher, from whom I have learned much. The mountain can explain all the tenets of Zen to those who wish to listen. One day I shall return to it so that it can test me once again.

I have come to love Mont Blanc. In its own way it has been good to me; it has certainly been good for me. It has not given me an easy time, but that is its Way. It is its only Way. It has not pretended to be other than what it is. After all, it is one of the great mountains. It has its reputation to protect; it must always be climbed with the utmost respect for its powerful forces. Otherwise climbers might show it too little consideration. Then they would experience its displeasure, a displeasure that I know can be awesome. Perhaps those who have died or been seriously hurt on Mont Blanc have not shown it sufficient respect. But that's something I'll never really know. It is the secret of the mountain and their secret; that at least they can share.

I also have shared in so much. Often pain, many times fear, eventually an explosion of joy, and ultimately a deeper understanding. It is so difficult to put into words everything I've learned on the mountain. Somehow I will have to try. I'll need to think it out quietly when I'm alone again. But the mountain is in no hurry, it is content to wait; it has all the time in the world.

My learning still continues; the teaching does not

end. I think that the answers that I've sought, that I've hoped to find, have in fact been given. But it will take me an indeterminate length of time, a change in my way of thinking, before I can hope to understand what these answers are and what they might mean.

I now know some things are neither true nor untrue, often neither black nor white, yet sometimes both. It is always vital to reach for the absolute. Zen can be a force and an inspiration, in every activity, in many ways. It creates an opportunity to reach out for the heights; it allows an individual to attempt, to obtain, the Summits of their own personal mountains. Mont Blanc was my mountain, but there are many other mountains out there, mountains of different colours and forms, waiting for those who are brave enough, those who are prepared enough, to take on their challenges.

MY HIGHLY RECOMMENDED ZEN AND MOUNTAIN BIBLIOGRAPHY

Alpine Climbing by John Barry (The Crowood Press 1988)

Chamonix Mont-Blanc by Max Chamson, Gaston Rébuffat, Roland Ravanel (Les Grands Vents 1983)

Modern Rock And Ice Climbing by Bill Birkett (A & C Black Publishers 1988)

Rain Sun Snow Hail Mist Calm by Andy Goldsworthy (Henry Moore Centre 1985)

The Handbook of Climbing by Allen Fyffe and Iain Peter (Pelham Books 1990)

A Primer of Soto Zen by Zen Master Dogen (East-West Center Press 1971)

Direct Pointing To Reality by Anne Bancroft (Thames & Hudson 1979)

Idle Jottings by Yoshida Kenko (Empty Circle Press 1988)

One Arrow, One Life by Kenneth Kushner (Arkana 1988)

Pointers To Insight by Sōkō Morinaga Roshi (The Zen Centre 1985)

Studies in Zen by Daisetz Suzuki (George Allen & Unwin 1960)

The Way Of Zen by Alan Watts (Thames & Hudson 1957)

Zen And The Ways by Trevor Leggett (Routledge & Kegan Paul 1978)

Zen Essence by Thomas Cleary (Editor) (Shambala Publications 1989)

Zen In The Art of Archery by Eugen Herrigel (Routledge & Kegan Paul 1953)